# The Education Revolution

*You say you want a revolution*

—*John Lennon & Paul McCartney*

# The Education Revolution

How to Apply
Brain Science to Improve
Instruction and School Climate

**Horacio Sanchez**

CORWIN
A SAGE Publishing Company

**FOR INFORMATION:**

Corwin

A SAGE Company

2455 Teller Road

Thousand Oaks, California 91320

(800) 233-9936

www.corwin.com

SAGE Publications Ltd.

1 Oliver's Yard

55 City Road

London EC1Y 1SP

United Kingdom

SAGE Publications India Pvt. Ltd.

B 1/I 1 Mohan Cooperative Industrial Area

Mathura Road, New Delhi 110 044

India

SAGE Publications Asia-Pacific Pte. Ltd.

3 Church Street

#10-04 Samsung Hub

Singapore 049483

Senior Acquisitions Editor:   Jessica Allan

Senior Associate Editor:   Kimberly Greenberg

Editorial Assistant:   Katie Crilley

Production Editor:   Laura Barrett

Copy Editor:   Deanna Noga

Typesetter:   C&M Digitals (P) Ltd.

Proofreader:   Ellen Howard

Indexer:   Beth Nauman-Montana

Cover Designer:   Gail Buschman

Marketing Manager:   Jill S. Margulies

Printed in the United States of America

*Library of Congress Cataloging-in-Publication Data*

Names: Sanchez, Horacio, author.

Title: The education revolution : how to apply brain science to improve instruction and school climate / Horacio Sanchez.

Description: Thousand Oaks, California : Corwin, a Sage Company, [2017] |

Includes bibliographical references and index.

Identifiers: LCCN 2016011756 |
ISBN 9781506332062 (pbk. : acid-free paper)

Subjects: LCSH: Cognitive learning. | Cognitive neuroscience. | Behavior modification. | School environment.

Classification: LCC LB1062 .S3117 2017 | DDC 370.15/2–dc23
LC record available at https://lccn.loc.gov/2016011756

This book is printed on acid-free paper.

16 17 18 19 20 10 9 8 7 6 5 4 3 2 1

# Contents

# Publisher's Acknowledgments

Corwin gratefully acknowledges the contributions of the following reviewers:

Melody L. Aldrich
Secondary High School Teacher
Casa Grande Union High School
San Tan Valley, AZ

Dara Feldman
Educational Consultant
Kensington, MD

Kendra Hanzlik
Instructional Coach
Prairie Hill Elementary School, College Community School District
Cedar Rapids, IA

# About the Author

 **Horacio Sanchez** is the President and CEO of Resiliency Inc., an agency leader in helping schools improve school climate, instruction, and discipline. Horacio is recognized as one of the nation's prominent experts on promoting student resiliency and applying brain science to improve school outcomes. The Maladaptive Council recognizes him as a leading authority on emotional disorders and resiliency. He is a highly sought-after speaker and has keynoted many regional and national conferences.

Horacio has been a teacher, administrator, mental health director, and consultant to the Department of Education in North Carolina, Pennsylvania, and other states. His diverse education and background have helped him merge research, science, and practice. He has authored several articles and books on the topics of resiliency, closing the achievement gap, and applying neuroscience to improve educational practices and outcomes.

# Introduction

*The loss of motivation to learn is not simply about academic success. The human brain is designed to reward learning, not because of academic pursuits, but rather to survive. . . . A healthy brain is designed to maintain and fine-tune by consistently learning new things on a daily basis. Therefore, students who have lost the motivation to learn are more likely to fail not only in school, but also in life. Their health depends on the wonderful transformation that is induced by daily learning.*

**T**his excerpt is but one example of how this book utilizes the current findings in neurobiology to help reveal how the brain learns and why behaviors occur. A pervasive issue when attempting to apply current brain research to behavior and learning is that the two disciplines primarily conducting these studies, neurology and psychology, often focus on unrelated issues. Very little of neuroscience focuses on learning; rather, it is often narrowly focused on cell and chemical function. Psychology often focuses on therapies and behavioral change through prescriptive behavior modification approaches. School psychologists familiar with education struggle to translate psychological assessments in a way that is meaningful to instruction or behavior management in the classroom. Therefore, after all the advancements in brain science and psychology, both disciplines have yet to enter the classroom. This book is timely because, although the topic has been pervasive, it seldom rises above the level of theory or enters the realm of application to truly help teachers apply the latest findings in brain research and psychology. This book synthesizes the current and most relevant findings in neuroscience and psychology and explains not only how they impact education but also how they can be applied within the classroom and school wide.

The first half of the book describes specific teaching strategies applying brain research. For example, incorporating physical movement into a lesson helps the brain understand abstract concepts. Later chapters look at how the most recent research on neurobiology can guide teachers in better utilizing any curriculum to meet desired outcomes. Teachers are provided specific steps that can enhance the structure and content in a curriculum to more effectively advance the academic performance of all students. How to better utilize curriculum is important because one of the current trends in course design has teachers placing an emphasis on higher-level learning goals. The problem is that the structure of most curricula is presented in a manner that reduces the likelihood that students will achieve higher-level thinking objectives and that results in frustrated teachers and students.

Frustrated teachers cannot perform at their best, and frustrated students lose the motivation to learn and are at greater risk of engaging in negative behaviors. For example, when students answer questions incorrectly, they do not receive the dopamine reinforcement associated with a correct response. A dopamine response creates the motivation for students to keep striving to continually get answers correct. Therefore, student success is the key to restoring motivation. Any book on instruction written within the current academic climate needs to address how to restore student motivation. The best instructional strategies will fail if students are unmotivated to learn. This book explains how the loss of motivation is increasing and how it can be overcome.

Another byproduct of today's educational climate is an increase in negative behaviors. Some of this can be attributed to increased interaction with technology. Many teachers are aware of the role technology is playing in negative behaviors such as cyberbullying, but few educators realize that it is also reshaping the human brain to be less able to focus and more callous toward the feelings of others. Teachers are clamoring for better ways to increase student focus and to manage the wave of negative behaviors they face daily. This book provides teachers with improved strategies for preventing and addressing negative behaviors. The unique approach presented provides validated strategies proven to be effective with even the most resistant students.

The human brain comprehends new information most readily when it can quickly associate it to prior knowledge. Authors and teachers are constantly walking the fine line between making new information understandable and simplifying it to the point that it fails to address challenging subject matter. One of the goals of this book is to review advancements in neuroscience that can be applied to the field of education and offer solutions to common education challenges. While every effort is made to discuss the science in laymen's terms, certain neuroscientific terms and theories are unavoidable. Be aware that the brain struggles with new terms and concepts because the association of new information without reference to prior knowledge is slower. Thus, educators should anticipate that the sections of this book that address familiar topics will be easier to comprehend; however, diligent review of the more challenging passages found in the first half of the book will enable each reader to obtain an increased level of assimilation.

The second half of the book shows teachers how to apply the latest findings in neurobiology to address the range of negative behaviors plaguing schools today. The emphasis throughout the book is on making abstract science concrete. Many resources on similar topics dedicate an inordinate amount of time to merely explaining problems. However, what teachers want most are solutions that help them improve student achievement, restore students' desire to learn, and manage student behavior.

Why the call for an educational revolution? A revolution is a fundamental change in organizational structures that takes place in a relatively short period of time. Many of the issues addressed in this book are vital not only to the education of our youth but also to their physical, social, and emotional well-being. When the changes identified can so dramatically improve the quality of life of each child, then quick, decisive action is warranted.

# A Brain-Based Approach to Teaching

Fuse/Thinkstock/Thinkstock

## THIS CHAPTER

The success of many lessons is often determined at the point of introduction. This is because the brain reacts poorly to new information when it is difficult to comprehend. Strategies in this chapter will improve students' abilities to consider and comprehend new information, increase information entry into short-term memory, and promote the perception that the information is relevant to their lives.

## THE BIOLOGY OF THE LEARNING BRAIN

Little is written concerning approaches to curriculum implementation and its correlation to effective outcomes and practices. For example, are the methods of instruction being implemented able to advance learning of a range of students from the gifted to the troubled student? The reality is that pathology is a direct result of altered brain function resulting from biological and environmental factors. Altered brain function has a direct correlation to how one is able to learn and retain lessons. A solution is utilizing an instructional approach that is compatible with how the brain learns most readily.

Optimal brain functioning occurs when chemical secretions in the brain are in balance—homeostasis. When not in balance, the brain is less able to manage new information. What is not common knowledge is that when new information is difficult to comprehend or contradicts prior learning, the brain's chemical response jeopardizes homeostasis. The brain processes information through cells called *neurons*. Emotion signals the neurons to send messages chemically. It is the efficiency of this process that predicts comprehension. Neurotransmitters send little sacks of chemicals and spew the contents to neuroreceptors (also called *dendrites*) that receive the information. One neuron can communicate with as many as 20,000 others. The brain has 100 billion neurons, and they all have the capacity to communicate with 20,000 other neurons, making learning a complex process.

A healthy brain knows when to send chemical messages, how much and which chemical to send, and how to process each chemical to produce an action. Basically, this chemical process accounts for everything an individual does and explains why learning deficits, as well as pathologies, can be summed up as abnormal brain chemistry. Damage to neurotransmitters or neuroreceptors will produce abnormal chemical levels in the brain, which result in atypical learning. Neurotransmitters and neuroreceptors can be damaged in a range of ways. One can inherit damaged neurotransmitters and neuroreceptors. Neurotransmitter and neuroreceptor impairments can also be caused by persistent exposure to stress or traumatic experiences. Even temporary periods of stress hinder learning until homeostasis is restored. Early deprivation from crucial stimuli that children require during the first few years of life can also alter neurotransmitter and neuroreceptor functions. However, what is not widely known is that exposure to fundamental stimuli during the adolescent brain rewiring process is also essential. What students engage in during puberty is highly predictive of the brain's later capacity.

When students are not chemically balanced, it will impact their entire physical system: heart, blood vessels, lungs, skin, salivary glands, muscles, digestion, and immune system (Chiras, 2012). Individuals who suffer from learning disorders or pathologies suffer from persistent chemical imbalance. For example, children who exhibit aggression often suffer from a serotonin imbalance. However, less widely known is that any abnormal secretions of any chemicals in the brain will impact learning temporarily or long term. Healthy students can go through a stressful period in their lives and experience issues with memory and comprehension similar to peers with persistent chemical imbalances. The difference is that for healthy students, the impact is only temporary. However, it is important for teachers to understand that temporary imbalances should be tended to and not ignored. The longer any chemical imbalance exists, the more difficult it will be to rectify.

The brain stem, the back region of the brain, regulates the body's homeostasis. This regulation is done through the autonomic nervous system, which extends throughout our entire body and regulates heart rate, respiratory rate, and digestion. The autonomic nervous system has two parts: The sympathetic nervous system alerts us through chemical arousal, and the parasympathetic nervous system calms us. When we experience chemical imbalance, the sympathetic nervous system can trigger stress, anger and irrational behavior. On the other hand, a chemical imbalance can cause the parasympathetic nervous system to make us feel lethargic, bored, and even depressed. To maintain homeostasis, our brain must feel safe and strike a delicate balance of not being overstimulated or disinterested.

Altered secretion patterns impact not only the back region of the brain, but also the midbrain that controls eating and sleeping. The midbrain is commonly referred to as the *limbic system* and is comprised of the hypothalamus, amygdala, and hippocampus. The amygdala determines emotional response, which can impact all bodily functions, especially eating and sleeping. That is why when individuals experience stress such as divorce, deadlines at work, or death of a loved one, they often experience temporary disturbances in their eating and sleeping patterns. The impact of chemical imbalance on the midbrain explains

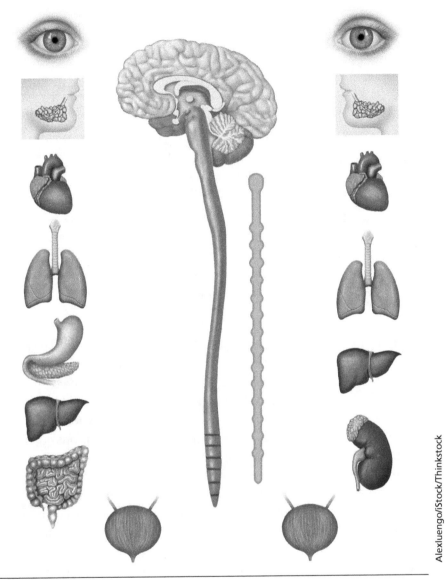

Alexluengo/iStock/Thinkstock

The brain impacts how the body functions

why so many psychiatric diagnoses co-occur with altered eating and sleeping patterns.

The impact of altered brain chemistry on the midbrain will have a ripple effect on the brain's entire system. The limbic system is known as the seat of human emotions, and it tells us when to run or fight. In simple terms, it is how the body reacts to danger, real or perceived. Before the limbic system responds to a stimulus, it consults with the cortex. The cortex is

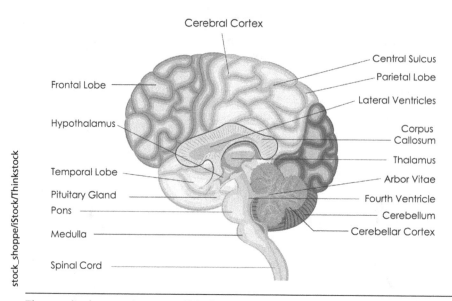

The cerebral cortex is responsible for executive functions.

in charge of reasoning and executive functions. The cortex takes in data and searches for related information to help individuals reach a reasonable decision based on prior experience. After analyzing data, the cortex communicates with the limbic system to justify or to reduce the level of emotional response. However, if chemical secretions overwhelm the limbic system, it will override the cortex and make impulsive decisions on its own. *It is this level of impulsivity and misperception that causes many children suffering from emotional problems to behave in a manner that is irrational.*

Altered secretion patterns impact not only behavior but learning as well. An essential component of the limbic system is the hippocampus; it is the seat of initial learning and short-term memory. A chemical imbalance slows initial learning and halts long-term learning, because long-term memory cannot exist unless preceded by short-term memory. Altered sleeping and eating patterns also impair the ability of the cortex to behave in a logical fashion. When the cortex is impeded, the ability to reason and problem solve is diminished.

The inability of the brain to appropriately manage some of the chemicals it produces causes it to function consistently outside of optimal learning conditions. Children whose brains are unable to control their bodies' chemical patterns are often the same individuals who experience mounting risk factors. The increased level of risk results in dramatic shifts in brain chemistry.

An understanding of how the brain learns should be reflected in every teaching process and practice to help at-risk students receive information in a manner that improves their brains' levels of functioning. Learning how the brain works is one of the most valuable pieces of information a teacher can acquire, and it can have positive ramifications on student performance regardless of level of risk. One of the best things about the human brain is that it is akin to the human heart. Most of the things that are good for one heart are good for all hearts, and most of the strategies that help one brain learn help all brains learn. When teachers learn strategies that are brain-compatible and gain a level of comfort utilizing strategies, instruction will become effective across cognitive abilities. Likewise, the process of learning is the secret to achieving a healthier brain. Learning is actually therapeutic.

## THE IMPORTANCE OF THE RELATIONSHIP WITH THE INSTRUCTOR

There is one caveat concerning maximizing brain-based strategies for enhancing learning. The ability of the teacher to build rapport with students cannot be replaced. Each brain-based strategy will provide the instructor with an effective tool for maximizing learning. However, research indicates that unless the strategy is delivered by a teacher who knows how to forge a positive relationship with students, the full benefit of each strategy cannot be obtained. Resiliency studies indicate that individuals who overcame the presence of multiple risk factors did so through a nurturing relationship with at least one adult. Numerous studies determined that the relationship between teacher and student is a predictor of whether or not the student will reach his or her potential. It is interesting to note that a myriad of studies on mental health treatment reached the same conclusion. The predictor of the effectiveness of treatment is the relationship between client and provider.

Therefore, it is only rational that the process for developing any curriculum must include an educational paradigm that effectively utilizes all of what is known about how individuals learn. The brain learns and applies information best when it is at its optimal level of functioning. There are some simple strategies that improve the brain's ability to receive new information. However, the strategies still require a caring and passionate teacher to deliver the lesson.

## STRATEGIES THAT PREPARE THE BRAIN TO LEARN

Help students feel at ease with new information. Effective instruction employs practices that reduce a student's production of chemicals that inhibit the brain's ability to function at its best. Teachers can learn to utilize techniques that help students relax before they are challenged.

### Beginning Class Ritual

Effective teachers often begin classes with the same ritual each day. The students grow accustomed to the routine and the predictability of the practice and thus learn to relax. This predictability helps the brain perform at its optimal chemical level or, at the very least, it will not increase chemicals that can hinder brain functioning. For example, some teachers use an interactive chant that incorporates positive affirmation with physical movement and unique sounds. A teacher, after watching the movie *300*, which is about an army of Spartans who overcame overwhelming odds, came into class one morning and told his inner-city high school class that they are like modern day Spartans and showed a clip from the movie. He told the students that they, too, have to overcome odds daily to survive, and one way of surviving is through education. So each morning he had his students engage in a warrior chant:

He would say, *"Are my warriors ready?"*

They would say, *"Ready,"*

He would say, *"What will my warriors do today?"*

They would say, *"Win."*

He would say, *"How can we win today?"*

The students will respond, *"Learn"* and let out a warrior *yell!*

He convinced his students that one way to win was overcoming the odds through education.

### Student Comfort

Other educators seek to create student *safety* by emphasizing what students have in common with one another. For instance, every Monday morning, a teacher would poll his students. The poll was a way of finding commonalities related to everyday activities such as how students' spent their free time, what they watched on television, or what types of music they listened to. Each time he would end the poll with the same phrase, *"You see, we are all unique, yet very much the same—uniquely the same."*

### Icebreakers

Another technique that can be utilized is icebreakers, which are an activity or game used to welcome and ease participants into a conversation. Although icebreakers are often traditionally used in meetings, training, or team building, they are just as effective as an everyday classroom tool. Icebreakers allow the students an opportunity to get in the right frame of mind to learn. Many students come to class with a lot on their minds, physically fatigued, and even stressed by personal issues. Brain research tells us that we cannot begin to engage the cortex, the location in the brain where new information is processed, until the need for safety and comfort are met. The cortex of the brain, the "higher" brain, is composed of many lobes specializing in complex functions: The occipital lobes primarily engage in visual processing; parietal lobes evaluate information about the body; temporal lobes, auditory analyses and memory; frontal lobes, reasoning and decision making. These primary functions have many complex facets, and no part of the cortex operates independently of the rest of the brain. Without comfort, the higher-ordered functions of the cortex are compromised. Comfort, in this case, is both physical and social.

Icebreakers should be fun. Humor has a very positive effect on the brain's chemistry. Some teachers begin class with a joke. It is very common to attend a conference and have the keynote speaker begin his or her talk with a joke. The reasons are far more brain-based than people imagine. When you laugh, the brain secretes hormones that not only relax us but also allow us to be open to new ideas. A positive frame of mind helps the brain consider new ideas without passing quick judgement. On the other hand, many of us can remember experiences in which the speaker said something that irritated us early in the lecture and we were closed off to everything else he or she had to say.

The beginning of class is not the time to challenge the students. It is important to remember that before you can challenge, you must first make safe.

## TECHNIQUES FOR INTRODUCING NEW SUBJECT MATTER

The learning of any new information causes increased chemical activity in the brain. The following strategies are designed to improve comprehension of new information without jeopardizing homeostasis. The greater the level of chemical disturbance to the brain during the learning process, the lower the comprehension and the higher the risk of impulsive student behavior.

## Correlate New Information to Prior Knowledge

Fundamentally, memory represents who we are. Our habits, our ideologies, our hopes, and fears are all influenced by what we remember of our past. At the most basic level, we remember because the connections between our brain's neurons change. Each experience primes the brain for the next experience, so every structural change in our brain reflects our history as a tree's rings tell the story from seed to towering oak. Memory also represents a change in who we are because it is predictive of what we will most likely focus on in the future. We remember new things more easily if we have been exposed to similar things in the past—so what we remember from the past has a lot to do with what we will learn in the future.

Another technique for keeping students relaxed when introducing new challenging information is to relate it to their past experiences. This technique is also essential for establishing lasting memories. Information does not get into long-term memory until it finds a connection to prior knowledge. Meaning in the brain can be described as the communication of a neuron with an existing cluster of actively communicating neurons dedicated to an area of learning. *Active* is defined in this context as neurons that have been communicating with each other so consistently that chemical exchange is efficient. Efficient communication between neurons means that the information can be effortlessly retrieved and related new information can be easily associated.

A dedicated function in the brain means that neurons are concerned with the carrying out of particular tasks. For example, if a child were to begin to play a musical instrument, the dedicated music neurons in the brain will become active. With practice and improvement, the communication between this set of neurons will become more efficient. If the child develops a high level of music proficiency, the number of dedicated neurons will increase. The rich network of neurons is more capable of making connections between new things learned and music. In addition, brain functions located in the region primarily involved in learning music will also benefit, which is why actively playing music has been consistently found to improve focus and spatial reasoning. The more you know about any subject matter, the more likely it will be to connect to related learning and eventually to unrelated information. For example, an economist views the world news through the lens of economics. The economist automatically associates world news to how the events impact the stock markets or currencies across the globe.

## Correlate New Information Through Shared Language

One simple technique to improve students' comfort with new information is using shared language. Imagine being in a classroom where all the students speak only English and the teacher only speaks French. No learning would transpire because the information would have no meaning. It is the teachers' job to present the information in a manner that every participant can understand. One way to achieve this goal is to have students explain new information in their own words. Other students might relate better to the manner in which one of their peers expresses the new information. This practice is a form of *formative assessment*, which allows the teacher to check the accuracy of student understanding. However, it is important that student perceptions are consistently monitored for accuracy to prevent the sharing of miscomprehension.

## Relate Information to Students Lives

Teachers can improve comprehension with new information by helping students realize how the material relates to their lives. In a popular movie, an English teacher attempts to demonstrate to her students that a classic work of literature relates to their lives. The teacher asks them to stand up if they had experienced any of the events that she describes. Once she had all students standing, she had them look around to see how many of them already related to the experience the author was describing. Individuals are likely to learn information that connects to emotional experiences. A simple technique for achieving this is through association—for example, associating a key point to a picture, song, or movie. Often images or popular songs conjure up emotions students experienced when watching the scene or listening to the song. Emotion is vital to the learning process because it triggers focus and activates increased regions of the brain (this concept is expanded on later in this chapter). However, a word of caution: The correlation of new information to strong negative emotions can result in an emotional shift for some students that can impede learning.

## Relate New Information to Pop Culture

There is an alternative strategy that allows teachers to connect to prior knowledge that is not dependent on knowing each student specifically but rather on keeping abreast of popular culture and social trends that have captured the attention and imagination of students. Certain trends are so prevalent that awareness transcends personal experience. For example, most teens today have a unique concept of the number symbol. They would primarily understand it as a hashtag used in social media to find themes or content. A hashtag before a word or phrase enables them to search all related comments made on a certain topic. Hashtags help social media determine when a topic is trending by compiling all the comments made. Hashtagging is so common to teens that they are aware of its meaning and significance even if they have never searched or posted a hashtag. Instruction can incorporate transcendent popular themes that encompass students' daily lives. The reference to this type of knowledge is effective because a majority of students will share a similar level of understanding.

Each year new things present as trends in the daily lives of students. Effective instruction can capitalize on this type of knowledge whenever possible. Teachers who take time to communicate with students concerning their lives can keep abreast of these trends with minimal effort. It is important to note that many trends last for brief periods in the lives of students and seldom are identified by them as significant—they come and go just like fashion trends. Therefore, it is important that teachers stay abreast of new trends when utilizing this technique, or they might sound dated.

## BRAIN-BASED STRATEGIES FOR IMPROVING RECALL

Instructors can attempt to ensure that new information is presented in a manner that increases entry into short-term memory. As mentioned previously, no information can make it into long-term memory unless it is first stored in immediate memory and then in short-term memory. Recent advancements in brain-based instruction have provided some techniques that have been proven to improve short-term memory retention. Teachers can use and modify these strategies to improve recall. These techniques are presented in this chapter and throughout the book; however, the primary key for successful use of these strategies is to apply them consistently.

The immediate goal of utilizing brain-based strategies is to increase entrance into short-term memory. However, the ultimate goal is to help short-term memories become long-term memories. The conversion of short-term memory to long-term memory is called *consolidation*. Consolidation is achieved through two processes. The first is synaptic consolidation—the early stage of making a long-term memory, which is a rapid process occurring within minutes to hours. The second is the systems consolidation process, which is the latter stage of making a long-term memory that can take weeks. The systems consolidation process allows short-term memories to become independent of the hippocampus by transferring information to the cerebral cortex where it will be stored as a long-term memory. Systems consolidation can be expedited from weeks into hours if new memories can be placed in an existing framework of knowledge. For example, you learn a new cooking recipe and immediately think of how the strategies employed in the newly learned recipe could enhance two dishes you make frequently. The assimilation of the new information into a well-established framework of knowledge expedites permanence.

Neurogenesis is the term used in neuroscience to describe the regeneration of brain cells. It is important to note that neurogenesis in the hippocampus is intimately related to systems consolidation (the making of long-term memories). The newly created cells are highly involved in new learning and transitioning information into long-term memory. Sharp-wave ripple complexes (SWRC), which were discovered through electroencephalograms (EEGs), provide evidence that interaction between the hippocampus and cerebral cortex produce long-term memory by the hippocampal replaying information while an individual sleeps or during quiet awake states. This discovery is further evidence that the brain requires repetition to achieve long-term memories.

## Create an Emotional Experience

There is an optimal level of emotion that is necessary for increased learning. Too much or too little reduces the efficiency of the cortex. This is why movies, books, and music that trigger emotions are easily remembered. The best lessons in life or in a classroom make you laugh, think, or cry. One of my high school teachers removed all the furniture from the classroom and taped small square dimensions on the floor that represented the amount of space a slave was afforded on the ships transporting them from Africa to America. During that lesson, students were seated tightly packed in their allotted squares for the duration of the period. We struggled to make it through the entire period and wondered how slaves could be in similar positions for months. My high school history teacher created an emotional experience that I remember vividly to this day.

If the movie, book, or lesson triggers memories associated with a traumatic experience, it can overstimulate the brain, reducing the learning process for certain students. The brain also increases learning when new information creates an experience. *Experience* here is best defined as the brain's becoming aware that the emotional system is in operation. Emotional words often trigger related past experiences to provide a deeper level of comprehension. However, this process usually happens in milliseconds and at a subconscious level. Humans remember for a longer time the events that elicit emotions (LeDoux, 1996).

It is important to understand the role that emotion plays in learning. It is biologically impossible to learn without emotion because emotion drives our attention system. Unless an individual focuses on new information, it cannot even enter immediate, much less short-term, memory. Once our attention is focused, the brain will store the information in immediate memory until its importance is determined. If it is important enough to the brain, it will enter short-term memory. Short-term memory will store items for 10 to 20 minutes. If the information finds meaning by being connected to prior knowledge, it will enter initial long-term memory. It is, therefore, crucial that teachers be masters at triggering emotion when introducing new information and during instruction. Well-designed lessons consistently trigger emotions at a subconscious level and conscious emotion when introducing a key point. Emotion causes different regions of the brain to fire at the same time. A well-accepted adage of the human brain is *what fires together wires together*. This means that emotion increases not only the ways memories can be retrieved but also the likelihood that the memory enters long-term memory.

## Example of Utilizing Emotion

After students are relaxed and new information is introduced in a nonthreatening manner, it is important that instruction captures students' attention by creating an emotional experience. For example, introduce a history section on the Vietnam War with a film that covers the three areas that will be covered: what the war was like, what was going on at home, and what soldiers experienced when they returned. The film allows the students to see the faces of the soldiers, promoting empathy because so many individuals drafted into the military were teenagers who had just completed high school. Empathy works in the brain by making connections to experiences that trigger similar emotions. This connection allows the brain to make instant associations improving short-term memory and increasing the likelihood for long-term recall. The film utilizes music to impact the heart and blood rate, deepening the emotional experience. Increased blood flow to the brain means more energy and oxygen improving the brain's overall performance. This introduction to the Vietnam War captures students' interests on a range of emotional levels sparking focus and the desire to learn more. Since emotion tends to produce stronger memories, the introduction to the Vietnam War provides a foundation that related new information will connect to more readily.

### Rote Rehearsal and Chunking

There are many methods that increase the probability of new information getting into short-term memory. Rote rehearsal is the repeating of information over and over again. It should be a natural conclusion that since the hippocampus consolidates short-term memories into long-term memories through repetition, that instruction embraces the same approach. New information is stored in working memory for only 15 to 20 seconds without rehearsal or constant attention (McGee & Wilson, 1984). The limitations of working memory can be somewhat circumvented by the ability to "chunk" information. Chunking is the presenting of information in small bits to assist the working memory's capacity for recall. A chunk is a grouping of information in which no cluster exceeds three to five items in a sequence. The most recognizable example of chunking is a standard phone number. Rather than 9195553290, it is presented as 919-555-3290. Later in this book *chunking* is referred to as a catchphrase. Studies on short-term memory reveal that it is difficult for the brain to retain large chunks of language (Gobet & Simon, 1998). A common strategy developed to improve instant recall is to reduce key information to small groups of words that are consistently repeated in the same order. Most individuals are conditioned to catchphrases' improving their recall because it is a common method utilized in advertisements. For example:

- A Coke and a Smile
- Just Do It
- Can't Eat Just One
- Finger-Licking Good
- The Ultimate Driving Machine
- Cuckoo for Coco Puffs
- Don't Leave Home Without It
- You Are in Good Hands
- Where's the Beef?

### Use Music

Utilizing music can also increase the probability that new information gets into short-term memory. As mentioned earlier, there are neurons in the brain that are dedicated to music. Information that is accompanied by music has the ability to increase the brain's focus. Many studies have shown the impact of music on recall. College students who consistently listened to Mozart's Sonata for Two Pianos in D Major demonstrated improved short-term memory and spatial reasoning (Rauscher, Shaw, &

Ky, 1993). Please note that music in this example did not make the students smarter; rather, it stimulated their ability to focus by listening to music prior to engaging in learning. Playing baroque music in the background increases students' ability to focus and comprehend (Sylvester, Voelkl, & Ellis, 2001). On the other hand, young children who take music lessons show different brain development and improved memory when compared to children who do not receive musical training. Musically trained children performed better on general intelligence tests in areas such as literacy, verbal memory, visuospatial processing, mathematics, and IQ (Fujioka, Ross, Kakigi, Pantev, & Trainor, 2006). Students who learn and consistently practice playing an instrument actually see an increase in white matter, the fatty myelin sheaths that encase the nerve fibers that connect one "thinking" area of the brain to another. Music is an important element in instruction. It provides a tool that will assist teachers in establishing a positive learning climate, a method to increase processing, and a technique to aid in recall.

## Utilize the Senses

Utilize as many senses as possible to improve recall. Each sense is processed slightly differently and stored in unique ways in the brain. A lesson that attacks two senses will have additional methods in which the information is stored as well as retrieved. For example, researchers have concluded that scientific breakthroughs have been expedited when scientists go beyond theories and calculations to hands-on trials. Something miraculous happens to the human brain's ability to learn and perform when it is engaged on a sensory level. Perhaps the greatest discovery of recent decades, that the DNA molecule is in the form of a three-dimensional double helix, would not have been unlocked unless Watson and Crick decided to use cardboard cutouts representing the individual chemical components and shifted them around as if putting together a puzzle. These two great minds concluded that it was their touching and moving these objects that had enabled their brains to solve the DNA puzzle.

Sensory stimulation explains why so many individuals remember significant meals and the events surrounding them. A great meal smells good, is visually appealing, tastes amazing, and requires motor movements. Every sense a meal utilizes is stored uniquely, and when recalling this experience, more regions are activated that can help in retrieval. It is logical that individuals naturally began to associate major events with a meal. Most holidays, weddings, and even funerals are commemorated with a meal. Human beings have subconsciously stamped certain events with this memory enhancer. Multisensory stimulation explains why traumatic events are hard to forget. Whenever you perceive that you are in danger, the brain heightens your senses. The result is that during traumatic events, individuals are more likely to remember sounds, smells, textures, tastes, and sights. This makes it hard to block out the memory, once a related sensory event is triggered.

## SUMMARY

Teaching can be viewed as two simple steps. First, introduce new information in a manner that will increase incorporation into short-term memory. When information is stored in short-term memory, it is increasing the efficiency of communication between two neurons. The first time two neurons communicate, the connection is weak and inefficient. Each time the process is repeated, the connection becomes stronger and more efficient. Storing information in an efficient manner means only that the data are stored in the brain, but they may not be easily retrievable. What is not easily retrievable is unlikely to be applied.

Second, connect new information to existing information. When a person has a wealth of knowledge on any topic, he or she possesses a cluster of neurons that are dedicated to storing, processing, retrieving, and applying related information. Once individuals have obtained a level of expertise in any area, they will naturally relate more events in life to their expertise. Dietitians see most diseases as health problems that can be prevented and managed through diet. Mathematicians utilize calculations to accomplish common daily tasks. Pastors perceive the world through the lens of their beliefs. Surveying students to identify their hobbies and interests is valuable. Put students with shared interests together to identify how the new information relates to their shared interest.

One of the most effective ways of creating an experience in a learning situation is by having students teach each other. This practice creates just enough emotional response to enhance memory, by relating information in the language of their peers, and by utilizing rehearsal to increase memory. Rehearsal is when an individual takes rote information and elaborates on it. Usually, rehearsal increases memory because it forces individuals to take the information and correlate it to what they know to explain it to others. This process allows students to put into practice what is being learned immediately. It is a well-accepted fact that one of the most efficient methods for improving internalization of information is doing something with the information within 24 to 48 hours of receiving it.

The human brain initially struggles when engaging in something new because it requires greater focus and effort. The natural tendency during the period of acquiring a new skill is to quit or revert to familiar methods because they are more automated. Teachers can overcome this tendency by identifying specific times or subjects when they will apply the strategies discussed in this chapter. Limiting the scope of the application allows teachers to focus more intensely for only short periods of time. Also, having set times to consistently practice the skills increases the speed of acquisition. Think about the time you were forced to learn a new software application because it was being installed in every computer across the district. Initially, you did not like the software, found it to be inefficient, and were often frustrated having to take the time to figure out a task you could complete quickly on the prior application. However, since you had to use the software daily, over time the application became easier and the advantages clearly seen. Think of these strategies as new advanced software that will improve student performance and outcomes. Each teacher must decide if he or she is willing to put in the effort required to gain proficiency and to experience the rewards identified through neuroscience or, instead, to retreat from the struggle to return to the familiar methods of instruction.

# Advanced Thinking
# Made Easy

2

Nastia11/iStock/Thinkstock

## THIS CHAPTER

This chapter explains the fundamental progression of learning. Essential information, referred to as *core information*, must achieve a level of automated recall for more advanced applications to be attained. This means repetition is essential at all levels of learning.

## WHAT LANGUAGE ACQUISITION TELLS US ABOUT LEARNING

The way people learn to talk remains the same no matter what age they are or when they begin to learn a language. This was the revolutionary finding of Harvard neuroscientists Jesse Snedeker, Joy Geren, and Carissa L. Shafto (2007).

The common belief in the 20th century was that children learn to talk by copying what they hear. The copycat theory cannot explain why toddlers are not partially fluent. If you listen to adults talk they do not often model one-word sentences: "beer," "TV," "remote" (unless we are talking about a football fans during football season).

In the past half century, scientists have developed additional theories about how children learn a language. The most popular one is the *mental development hypothesis*, which states that speech matches brain development much like a child must physically develop crawling before he or she is able to walk. The theory states that babies' brains are not developed enough to handle complex speech until their brains are ready. However, a huge hole was blown in this theory when Snedeker, Geren, and Shafto looked at 27 children ages 2 to 5 from China who were adopted by parents in the United States. Since these children were older when they began to learn English, their stage of brain development would allow them to produce more fluent speech more quickly. However, these 27 orphans still began with single words, dropping word endings, and not conjugating verbs. They still went through the same language stages as a typical American-born child. The Harvard neuroscientists concluded that baby talk is not a product of a less developed brain, but rather a lack of knowing a sufficient number of words.

This finding challenges the dated concept that age alone should determine what children are capable of learning. Two recent reports from the National Research Council indicated that children learn best when they regularly revisit topics, moving from basic to sophisticated. The Council suggests that core standards be identified at each grade level per subject and a strategy implemented for ongoing review of those elements to promote automation. These reports indicate that base understanding should be somewhat automated before individuals can engage in more advanced thinking. In other words, more complex sentences, grammar, and even creative expression can be produced at a younger age by children who have learned a larger number of words, if their word knowledge is automated. The research of Roy F. Baumeister showed that the brain is not good at multitasking. When humans are forced to do two things that require focus, both tasks will suffer. However, if one thing has repeatedly been done so that it is almost automated, then the brain can do the other task to a greater level of efficiency. The implication is that if a child is struggling to think of words, he or she cannot engage in syntax and creative expression.

The need for automation makes sense if one considers how the brain naturally learns. Repetition of any task improves the quality of the connections in the brain, thereby, creating more automated function. Think of how children learn the alphabet. The alphabet is actually a very advanced concept. There are 26 letters in the English alphabet. Each letter can be written in upper or lowercase, and each letter represents a unique corresponding sound. Even more confusing is that when letters are coupled together, their unique sounds can change. The ability to recognize letters and know their corresponding sound is fundamental (core) to learning words. Repetition is essential to achieving automation. Over time teachers found that students who learned the alphabet utilizing strategies that increased entry into short-term memory became proficient quicker. As a result, teachers have students recite the alphabet, sing the alphabet, make physical movements representing each letter in the alphabet, color the alphabet, write the alphabet, and recognize it in and out of sequence. Students who master the alphabet are able to transition from recognizing letters to words easily. Those who do not master the alphabet struggle because they work so hard to recognize letters and recall corresponding sounds that their brains cannot focus on the recognition of words and their meanings. It has been established that the brain learns by making associations and connecting new information with what is already learned. Therefore, advanced thinking is merely a function of the brain's having enough information to begin to make advanced associations.

Let's look at the implications of these findings on the ever-shifting extremes of education. There was a time when children learned certain facts at each grade level. These facts were drilled and became automated. Then someone made the observation that rote memorization is not advanced thinking, which is the goal of education. This caused an extreme shift in the educational landscape away from rote memorization such as learning vocabulary words, emphasizing correct spelling, and memorizing multiplication tables to focus on how to promote advanced thinking. We started teaching first graders to write freely and to not worry about spelling or punctuation, in hopes of creating the next Robert Frost. Although in this case, the new Robert Frost would have a limited vocabulary and would not spell or write legibly. Both approaches were flawed. Children need age-appropriate knowledge that has become automated; but if schools just engage in rote memorization, we do not help the brain make sophisticated associations. However, if we focus on advanced thinking and don't teach any foundation information, advanced thinking cannot occur.

*Advanced thinking* in this context is best defined as principles and concepts that students should be able to comprehend based on the core set of information that has been taught to a level of automation. As reflected in the alphabet example, if students master recognition of letters and their corresponding sounds, then they can advance to sounding out words and learning their meanings. Some students come from environments in which age-appropriate information is taught and utilized with great regularity. For example, some children are read to each night and become familiar with common themes of children's books. Others have parents who play math games and reinforce learning through everyday experiences such as, how many shoes are there? Now add Mom's shoes, and how many do you have? Some children are exposed to unique colors found in art, sounds in music, a wide range of tastes, and even the feel of interesting textures, which have been found to enhance learning. Students who are exposed to a variety of concepts and experiences are better capable of advanced thinking because their brains have prior knowledge and can make associations based on prior exposure. Students from less advantaged backgrounds cannot comprehend the same things because there is not the sufficient prior knowledge to gain comprehension, much less to move on to higher-level thinking.

So maybe this time the answer is in the middle and not in the extremes. Identify core knowledge related to each subject and drill it until ALL students possess this foundation. Then identify what are age-appropriate advanced concepts that can be obtained from this information. The National Research Council determined that a simple concept or principle that is introduced early results in greater advanced thinking in the future. Studies on individuals who became accomplished in their chosen fields reveal that early exposure along with high amounts of repetition of related core information as compared to their peers was the key difference. Genius is nothing more than learning a wealth of information in one area, and then being able to make sophisticated associations from a wide range of knowledge that results in the bringing of two ideas together that no one had previously connected.

For example, a teacher recently told me that the kindergarten curriculum in place at her school allocates 4 weeks for measurements and 2 weeks for addition and subtraction. However, for kindergartners, initial number recognition represents core information. If kindergartners are unable to quickly recognize numbers and their related values, advanced math concepts will be impossible to master. Once students' recognition of numbers is automated, then addition and subtraction are the next level of core information. The majority of elementary school math lessons are built on the foundation of addition and subtraction. Therefore, the above curriculum's structure is not brain compatible. A teacher who can identify core information across the kindergarten curriculum will quickly realize the need to spend more time on addition and subtraction while reducing the time alocated for measurements. In addtion, the teacher knows to periodically review addition and substraction through quick drills designed to increase the speed of recall. Automation requires a level of review over an extended period of time. This simple adjustment to the curriculum will increase students' success in future math lessons.

There are many ways teachers can identify core information. One approach is to work backward, identifying the higher-level thinking goals first. The second step is determining what concepts build on one another to prepare students to achieve the identified higher-ordered thinking outcomes. Third, is to determine what information is consistently utilized in all the concepts from simple to complex. The information that is consistently utlized is the core information. For example, if a higher-level thinking goal is the ability to compose a research paper, then the curriculum might focus on selecting a topic, researching, developing a thesis sentence, outlining, note organization, writing a first draft, editing, and a final paper. However, all these skills are built on the core information of paragraph development. No student can achieve this higher-level thinking goal without the ability to write a paragraph with little effort. If the brain has to expend a high degree of energy to develop each paragragh in the paper, it is likely that the student will avoid working on the paper. It is also likely that some students will require an earlier level of core information, such as sentence writing. A teacher who does not ensure that the majority of the students obtain a level of automation in sentence writing and then paragraph development will struggle to get all students to attain the advanced skills of writing a research paper. A consistent review of sentence writing and paragraph development while students learn to write a research paper will increase their achievement of this higher-level thinking goal.

## THE FOUNDATION OF LEARNING

The ability to identify core information is the foundation of advanced learning. Presenting core information utilizing brain-based strategies, which were introduced in Chapter 1, along with sufficient repetition is the key to automation and to the ability of students to progress as the curricula builds. Teachers can begin to improve student performance by first identifying the core information related to each section of the curriculum. Once core information is identifed, then provide sufficient opportunities for repetition of the core information to achieve automation. The utilization of brain-based strategies during the review process will help students attain automation in a more efficient manner. For example, students need to learn and remember the formula to calculate average speed: average speed = total distance/total time. In this case, the teacher will not have to chunk the information because the formula is already brief, but will determine if a visual cue, music, or movement can be used to improve recall. The teacher decides to assign the formula a symbol, a picture of a car that is not going too fast or too slow 🚗 to represent average speed, and use gestures to reflect distance and time. Whenever the class reviews the formula, the teacher displays the 🚗; students say, "Average speed;" extend both arms wide when they say, "Total distance;" and then tap the top of their wrist (where often a watch is worn) when they say, "Divided by total time." Grouping the formula with a visual cue and gestures will improve learning and recall.

Core information is any concrete fact that must be able to be recalled instantly to accomplish a learned skill. For example, to master the skill of driving, knowing which is the gas pedal and which is the brake pedal and how to apply each appropriately is considered core information. If your brain continued to work as hard to remember which is the gas and which is the brake as you did when you first began to drive, your ability to advance as a driver would be impossible. Neck jerking starts and sudden stops, as well as panic to apply the correct pedal when needed, would always be your primary focus. Students who fail to attain automation of required core information are quickly left behind, and concepts are layered and become more complex. This is why identifying core information and helping students attain automation is the foundation of future learning.

# Three Levels of Learning

ELENAPHOTOS/iStock/Thinkstock

## THIS CHAPTER

This chapter explains how neuroscience determined that learning occurs on three levels. The three levels are core information, principles and applications, and higher-level thinking. Chapter 3 provides an overview of why it is so essential that teachers are able to identify each of the three levels of learning and understand their independent functions. Chapters 4, 5, and 6 present a more in-depth review of each level of learning independently.

## INTRODUCTION

Learning can be broken down into three basic components: core information, principles and applications, and higher-level thinking. Teachers should consider these components when designing instruction. Before describing each of the three components in detail, it is important to know that there are two well-established premises that are the foundations of delivering instruction through the lens of the three levels of learning: the human brain cannot multitask, and learning is the process of helping the brain make continuious connections.

## THE FIRST PREMISE

The first premise is that the brain can focus only on one thing at a time. Earl Miller, professor of neuroscience at Massachusetts Institute of Technology (MIT), states, "People can't multitask very well, and when people say they can, they're deluding themselves" (Hamilton, 2008). When we think we are multitasking, the brain is actually switching from one task to the other task rapidly. He states that some tasks are almost impossible to do simultaneously, like writing an e-mail and talking on the phone at the same time. "You cannot focus on one while doing the other. That is because they both involve communicating via speech or the written word, and so there's a lot of conflict between the two tasks in the brain" (Hamilton, 2008). Magnetic resonance imaging shows that in cases of multitasking, the brain struggles to complete both tasks.

However, a very small portion of the population actually can multitask. David Strayer, director of the applied cognition lab at the University of Utah, studied multitaskers and determined that only 2 percent of the population can juggle two tasks efficiently (Medeiros-Ward, Watson, & Strayer, 2012). An even smaller segment of the population can truly manage multiple tasks. By this time, many of you reading this book have concluded that you are in the 2 percent. The more logical conclusion should be that you are in the 98 percent and are merely deceiving yourselves.

The rules for multitasking are as follows: One, the brain can do it best when both tasks have been done so frequently that the tasks are almost automated, and as long as the tasks do not occupy the same areas of the brain. However, the performance of both tasks will suffer slightly. This slight drop in performance is low enough that people often delude themselves into thinking that they are performing optimally. Rule 2, when doing one new task and one automated task, the brain will focus its energy on the new task. The final rule is that if both tasks are new, the brain will struggle to do both, often resulting in a level of chemical imbalance that impedes learning and performance.

## THE SECOND PREMISE

The second premise is that the brain learns by making connections. There are a few key rules concerning how the brain makes connections that impact student learning. The first rule is that the brain makes sophisticated connections while you sleep. Students with emotional disorders or those who are exposed to persistent stress will make fewer connections in their lifetimes than the typical person because both emotional disorders and exposure to stress negatively impact sleeping, resulting in fewer connections being made. Therefore, the achievement gap increases every night.

The achievement gap is something that has been debated. However, a scientific look at the issue seems to clarify its existence. For example, a healthy student gets 6 hours of rapid eye movement (REM) sleep each night. While in REM sleep, the brain does three basic functions: (1) repairs, (2) reinforces things learned that day, and (3) makes sophisticated connections producing high-level thinking. A student suffering from emotional issues or persistently exposed to stress spends a significantly lower amount of time in REM sleep. The result is fewer repairs, less reinforcement of things learned, and less sophisticated connections. Every night, students getting less sleep face a mounting gap with their peers. Over the course of several years, the gap becomes a chasm.

The second rule is that we tend to make the most connections to the subject matter at which we are the most adept. This means more things are connected to areas of expertise. Consider great cooks: when they view the world, it seems that they associate everything to the cooking experience or food. The negative finding here is that individuals who lack well-developed areas of knowledge will make fewer connections overall. In other words, *the smart get smarter*.

The third rule is that making associations to things people know well is least taxing to the human brain and is most likely to be understood.

Connecting new information to prior knowledge causes less chemical disturbance than when trying to learn novel information with no context. When the brain is able to maintain homeostasis, an individual retains the optimal state of mind for learning and is better prepared to consider more challenging ideas.

To review, there are two key premises, each with three rules. Premise 1, the brain can only focus on one thing at a time. The three rules related to Premise 1 are:

1. We multitask better when both tasks are automated.

2. When one task is automated and the other new, the brain will focus energy on the new task.

3. New tasks when done simultaneously will result in a considerable drop in performance.

Premise 2, the brain learns by making connections. The three rules related to the second premise are:

1. We make connections while we sleep.

2. We connect to things we are more adept at.

3. Associations to things we know well are the least taxing to the brain.

Before leaving this topic, it is important to mention the implications that the findings mentioned above have on the understanding of what genius is. *Genius* is best defined as an individual who has such a deep understanding of an area of expertise that he or she sees novel connections based on his or her life experiences. These connections are not evident to most of us because we lack the deep understanding and cannot make the same associations. However, there is another type of genius—the individual who possesses a supreme level of expertise in more than one area. Many times this genius is able to connect a deep level of understanding in two unrelated fields leading to radical breakthroughs. A prime example of this is Leonardo da Vinci—a painter possessing advanced skills as a sculptor, architect, musician, scientist, mathematician, engineer, inventor, anatomist, geologist, botanist, and writer. His advanced knowledge in so many disciplines allowed his mind to connect art, math, and engineering to envision inventions as advanced as a bicycle and even a flying machine. The point here is critical. Genius might require an element of intelligence, but at its core are the depth of understanding and the uniqueness of connections that have propelled humankind.

## CORE INFORMATION

The two above-mentioned premises clearly illustrate that all curricula build on core information. Core information is the first element of learning. *Core information* refers to the fundamental elements that must be automated for learning to take place. For example, in reading, the core information is phonemic awareness. If a student struggles to produce sounds, the brain will be unable to focus on words and comprehension. The goal with core information is to create rich networks of sensory input that fire simultaneously to produce long-term potentiation (LTP). LTP is a persistent increase in synaptic strength following the high-frequency stimulation of a chemical synapse. Learning and memory are possible thanks to the strengthening of synapses between nerve cells (Goold & Nicoll, 2010). This learning process begins in the hippocampus. The hippocampus is also responsible for coordinating all sensory input. It has been proven that when information stimulates multiple senses simultaneously, it improves not only recall but also the speed of recall. However, for automation to truly occur, repetition is required. Simply put, core information is best achieved by simultaneously stimulating multiple senses repeatedly.

## PRINCIPLES AND APPLICATIONS

The second element of learning is principles and applications. Principles and applications are basically what teachers want students to do with the core information. For example, a student who is taught phonemic awareness and grade-appropriate sight words can be asked to produce sentences, paragraphs, and even essays. However, the simple truth is that if a student has not mastered phonemic awareness and does not have an appropriate level of sight words, he or she will be unable to do these applications. The brain will work so hard on producing the words that sentence structure and meaning will suffer. Remember the rule: The brain will struggle to focus on two new things simultaneously (multitasking), which is why some core information related to every subject matter must be automated.

## HIGHER-LEVEL THINKING

The third element of learning is higher-level thinking. Higher-level thinking in an academic setting is the brain putting new information that has been taught together with prior knowledge. However, students who have not mastered core information to the point of automation will struggle to understand key concepts. Students who have mastered core information but have not experienced principles and applications through the aid of embodied cognition often are unable to make advanced connections. There has been a tendency to believe that students who fail to attain higher-level thinking objectives have limited cognitive capacity. However, it has been established that children at any age and within a broad range of aptitudes can engage in higher-level thinking as long as core information is automated and the applications have been learned utilizing many sensory inputs.

## STRATEGIES FOR IMPLEMENTING THE THREE LEVELS OF LEARNING IN A CLASSROOM SETTING

- Select a few core elements. Teach them in a manner that stimulates the senses simultaneously: movement, music, visuals, and manipulatives.
- Establish set times throughout the school year to quickly review core information. Remember, without core information being automated, students cannot achieve advanced learning.
- When students seek to apply what they have learned, make sure that the principles and applications allow for them to manipulate it in more ways than just verbal or written. For example, when applying what they have learned about sentence structure, give students cards that have parts of speech on them. Then let the students move the cards around trying out different combinations. Have students tap out the rhythm of a sentence structure. Allow them to draw the sequence of a sentence, watch videos on sentence composition, hear how others compose sentences, and play different games with sentences. The goal is for them to manipulate what they have learned until they reach a level of familiarity and comfort.
- Establish learning experiences that guide students to put what they have learned together without help. The teacher can take on the role of coach, setting up clever problems or situations for students. For example, if the higher-level thinking goal is to be able to produce expressive writing, the teacher could have a collection of sentences on strips of paper and explain that these sentences, when put together, tell a story and solve a mystery. The story can be put together many ways; the only limit is students' imaginations. Then, once the students achieve this, they can make their own story puzzle.

Look at each segment of the curriculum through the lens of the three elements of learning. If this is not done, students who are slow to obtain automation struggle to apply principles and will consistently fail to produce higher-level thinking objectives. A word of caution, more and more curricula are placing an emphasis on higher-level thinking objectives. Unless the teacher can determine what core information needs to be automated and what advanced skills need to be mastered, higher-level thinking cannot occur. The outcome is teachers spending more time on teaching advanced concepts and a discrete part of the student population never being able to comprehend no matter how many different ways the topics are approached. The science is clear, without automation of core information, advanced learning will be compromised.

In the next few chapters, we dig deeper into the concepts of core information, principles and applications, and higher-level thinking.

# Working Toward Automation—Core Information

Shironosov/iStock/Thinkstock

## THIS CHAPTER

This chapter explains why the automation of core information is decreasing among students and the negative impact it is having on education. Recommendations for developing an efficient review process are provided as well as strategies to help students attain automation in a shorter amount of time.

## THE DROP IN AUTOMATION

The desire for all students to engage in the most advanced academic thinking at each grade level is a noble one. If you ask any parent, Would you rather your child have an elementary understanding of the classics or a profound comprehension of the role that literature plays in cultivating thinking? almost every parent would pick higher-level thinking. It was this same sales pitch that transformed terms like *rogue memory* and *drilling* to equal educational profanity. The phrase *drill and kill* provides great insight about how public education allowed itself to be driven from its foundational roots by a campaign that had lofty goals without true comprehension of the learning process. No teachers worth their salt would waste their time drilling the multiplication tables when students could be solving the next great mystery beyond DNA.

The challenge is that the road map to creating minds capable of such brilliance actually requires automation of core information. What is automation in relation to the human brain? *Automation* in the human brain is best defined as a level of efficiency in recalling information that requires minimal energy. Because minimal energy is required for foundational elements, it allows the brain to focus its energies on advanced information by being able to forge new connections.

The human brain automatically achieves automation when a level of repetition occurs. Before scientists were able to look into the human brain while it was engaging in a process, automation was explained as information the brain determines is important as evident by the ease of recall. Through advancements in brain scanning, it is now known that repetition changes the structure of dendrite connections, improving efficiency. Once dendrite structures reach a certain point of transformation, they are further enhanced by a process called *myelination*, which adds greater efficiency to the chemical communication in the brain. Myelination not only adds to the efficiency of how chemical signals are processed in the brain, but it also reduces the risk that information will be easily forgotten.

Let's explore some reasons why automation has been lost in today's educational climate.

- First, teachers no longer drill information in the classroom. The reasons are numerous: Drilling is often considered as poor quality teaching, teachers are instructed to focus on higher-level thinking goals contained in the curriculum, and pacing guides often require teachers to cover all the material that will be included in end-of-year testing. These factors have convinced many teachers that they cannot afford to waste time with extensive reviews.

- Second, automation is now supposed to take place in the home. Many of the activities parents engage in with younger children, such as reading to them or using number flashcards, begin to prime the brain with a level of automation required for school preparedness. When students get older, homework is supposed to provide the repetition required to achieve automation of key information. However, many students do not do enough homework or do not engage in homework at all. The amount of homework being completed often does not meet the standard required for the brain to obtain automation. Further complicating the issue is that some schools do not give homework at all. Even schools that give a sufficient amount of homework often have a percentage of students who lack the necessary level of comprehension to complete the homework, and as a result, they too will not meet the level of repetition required to produce automation. Across the nation, many parents are being forced to seek additional academic supports to ensure that their children obtain a level of automation. Because the advanced science, math, and English homework assignments are beyond the ability of many parents to provide assistance, or due to time constraints, parents do not have the opportunity to provide consistent assistance.

It is not a stretch to conclude that one of the main reasons that academic scores are not improving at the levels predicted is that a majority of struggling students lack the level of automation required for comprehension of advanced subject matter. This issue is compounded by the fact that at each grade level, there is a level of core information that must be mastered in order to acquire the next set of core information. By the secondary levels in education, teachers are attempting to teach students who are not only missing some core information, but years of core information. In these situations, the task of teaching students the core information required to do grade-level work seems daunting. It has produced a crisis of confidence in schools with a concentration of students lacking a firm foundation of learning.

Many teachers engage in a review process only at the beginning and the end of the academic year. However, for the process of achieving automation, such an approach is counterproductive. It is ongoing bursts of repetition that changes the brain structure to produce automation. Teachers should consider the review at a dedicated time, limited to 5 minutes per subject matter daily. For example, if a section of the curriculum lasting 2 weeks mandates that students be able to recall six new terms and their meanings, then during that 2-week period, the teacher will review terms and definitions for the first 5 minutes of class each day.

For automation to truly be solidified, students cannot go through any extended period of time without recalling prior automated information. Initially review should be every few days, then weekly, then monthly. This means that the teacher must carefully design daily reviews that will produce automation of new material in the allotted time while rotating prior core information into the daily review process. For example, after spending 2 weeks reviewing the six new terms and their meanings, the next section of the curriculum requires students to be able to recall two formulas that will have to be put into practice throughout the remainder of the school year. The teacher will focus the review process on the automation of the two new formulas during the week but will weave the six terms learned earlier into the review process. This can be achieved by including a different term each day. Over time, the material introduced earlier will not have to occur as frequently but will never be completely omitted.

"I feel the need for speed." The famous line from the movie *Top Gun* is appropriate when discussing automation. The ability to increase the speed at which information is brought back is an indication that myelination is taking or has taken place. To facilitate myelination, teachers should introduce a rhythmic pace to the review process. A slower pace is utilized whenever students are initially reviewing the information. Once the students have become more familiar with the material, the teacher will increase the pace of the review. When students seem very comfortable with the material, the teacher goes even faster. For example, the teacher can tell the students that he or she will use a gesture cue to let the students know when to repeat information aloud. Once the students have become familiar with the material, the teachers says, "Since you all have been doing so well with the review, we are going to go a little faster today." In the final state of automation, students should no longer be struggling to recall the information. At that time, the teacher should challenge the students by saying, "Since you all have been doing so well, we are going to go even faster with our review today."

When multiple senses are stimulated along with the use of language, the odds of the information entering short-term memory is dramatically improved. It is well-accepted knowledge that initial learning takes place in the hippocampus. The hippocampus is considered part of the primitive brain structure that was present long before the human brain evolved to have a frontal region that we all know as the cortex. The cortex plays a significant role in rational decision making and the retention of formal learning. However, the hippocampus is responsible for short-term memory, and without entering short-term memory no long-term retention can occur in the cortex. Prior to the inception of language, the hippocampus processed only sensory input. The processing of language for entry into short-term memory is an evolved function of the hippocampus. Since the primary focus remains on sensory processing, the hippocampus actually does a poor job with language retention.

Two things can be done to improve the hippocampus's ability to retain language: shorten language input and stimulate as many sensory inputs simultaneously when introducing language. What does it mean to shorten language input? For example, when teaching the legal case *Brown v. Board of Education*, "separate but equal" was the legal doctrine in United States constitutional law that justified racial segregation based on the *Plessy v. Ferguson* decision in 1896. However, the doctrine was overturned by a series of Supreme Court decisions because of *Brown v. Board of Education* in 1954. The National Association for the Advancement of Colored People (NAACP), led by the soon-to-be first black Supreme Court Justice Thurgood Marshall, was successful in challenging the constitutional viability of the "separate but equal" doctrine. The Supreme Court voted to overturn 60 years of law, stating separate is not equal because it deprives people the equal protection under the laws guaranteed by the Fourteenth Amendment. The students will learn two distinct short phrases: The constitutional law for segregation based on *Plessy v. Ferguson* was *separate but equal*. The new law based on *Brown v. Board of Education* that put an end to segregation was *separate is not equal*. The two key phrases designed to limit the use of too many words are *separate but equal* and *separate is not equal*.

Core information is the distilling of key facts, formulas, and processes that have to be brought back quickly for a range of information to be comprehended and mastered. Getting students to be able to recall key information quickly is rudimentary to learning and cannot be dismissed as trivial. It is important that no one misunderstand that the call for automation of key information is a substitute for good instruction; rather, it is the foundation on which good instruction is built. A highly qualified teacher should be able to look at any curriculum and ascertain what core information is necessary if higher-level thinking goals are to be obtained.

There is an additional advantage gained by getting core information to the level of automation. When core information can be retrieved quickly, it aids the brain in bringing back other related learning. Many students who struggle academically retain information but fail to file it well in their brain. If a fact associated with a body of information is retrieved, it will improve the brain's capacity to bring back related learning. This has to do with the fact that the brain remains on one track and will continue to open related files until a person shifts to another train of thought. The brain's anterior cingulate cortex (ACC) explains why so many people begin to think about a problem and cannot seem to get it off of their minds. Until they truly shift to another line of thought, the brain will continue opening any related information. The ACC is especially involved when effort is needed to focus on a singular task. To keep the brain focused, the ACC keeps recalling related information. Teachers can actually tell students that once they bring back core information that they know well, the brain will help them bring back other things they learned related to that core information. This means that the more efficiently a student recalls core information, the more effective he or she will be in accessing related advanced concepts.

## LONG-TERM POTENTIATION

Once an efficient review process is in place and teachers learn how to skillfully distill key information to a small chunk of language, they still need to group a range of sensory strategies with that core information to expedite long-term potentiation (LTP). Remember, the hippocampus initially processed only sensory input. The advent of speech, which is safely estimated to have taken place between 200,000 to 2 million years ago, means that humans were on Earth without formal language for an extensive period of time (Johanson & Edgar, 1996). The earliest stone tools in archaeological records of our human ancestors date back 2.5 million years (Morgan et al., 2015). A well-accepted assumption is that humans were living and working in clans at least a half a million years before the inception of language. It is commonly believed that we did not go from no communication to the spoken word dramatically. Rather, we learned to maximize communication utilizing visuals, gestures, and sounds. Due to today's dependence on the spoken word, people often fail to realize that the hippocampus continues to process the language through the lens of sensory input. For example, we are influenced by facial expressions, voice inflections, and gestures to comprehend meaning in much of our communication.

The goal of the review process is to achieve LTP. In neuroscience, LTP is a long-lasting enhancement in signal transmission between two neurons that results from stimulating them synchronously (Cooke & Bliss, 2006). The key to achieving LTP is accepting that the hippocampus maximizes retention whenever sensory cues accompany the language.

A teacher can utilize a simple visual cue to represent each phrase. If one wants to understand the effectiveness of visual cues in increasing LTP, one has to look only at how logos are utilized in marketing. For instance, the peacock represents NBC. It has long been known that the human brain can associate information with a visual cue. What was not discovered until much later is the fact that students coming from stressful environments or suffering from a chemical imbalance due to emotional disorders might require visual cues to be able to learn. It seems that when the human brain is stressed, the focus on visuals is heightened. This is likely a survival adaptation. However, this means that teachers instructing in high-risk schools or in schools where there is a high concentration of poverty should maximize the use of visuals and visual cues during instruction.

The utilization of a visual cue with a chunk of information is no different from the use of a logo with a catchphrase. See if you can visualize the logos for the catchphrases below:

| | |
|---|---|
| A Coke and a Smile | |
| Just Do It | |
| Must Be the Shoes | |
| Think Different | |
| Truth in Engineering | |
| The Ultimate Driving Machine | |
| Can't Eat Just One | |
| Don't Leave Home Without It | |
| When it absolutely, positively has to be there overnight. | |
| When you care enough to send the very best. | |

Another common method for advancing LTP is by chunking language with gestures. In a study published in 2009, Jeremy Skipper and colleagues utilized discreet gestures as an instructional strategy, not only to explain a topic but to advance retention (Skipper, Golden-Meadow, Nusbaum, & Small, 2009). They found that when a problem is hard, hand movements activated the brain's problem-solving region. In addition, when the students gestured, it was found that their recall improved. Gestures reduce the cognitive load of new learning, leaving more brain-power available for remembering information. One does not have to be a researcher to verify these findings. One only has to think about any song you learned as a child that incorporated movement. It is very likely that you not only remember the movement, but the song as well.

There are two methods for introducing LTP elements for any review. One is straightforward: group all the elements together from the beginning, or scaffold the methods by introducing one then adding another. The example below illustrates how a lesson on the two parts of the primitive brain can be reduced to a catchphrase and how the strategies of visual cues and gestures can be layered.

## EXAMPLE

Today we are going to learn about two parts of the human brain. One part is called the amygdala. The amygdala is also part of the limbic system and is in the shape of an almond. So everyone make an almond shape like this:

An individual can be born with a damaged amygdala. In addition, the amygdala can be damaged by trauma, stress, and disease. It enables an individual to read the nonverbal cues of others: facial expressions, postures, gestures, and tone of voice. Its primary role is your survival. As a result, when it perceives that you are threatened, it takes over brain functions, so you act. So in many ways, your amygdala controls emotions. Can we all repeat the following phrase out loud while making the gesture for the amygdala?

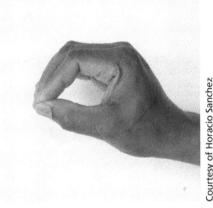

Courtesy of Horacio Sanchez

The amygdala controls emotions.

The next part of the brain we are going to learn about is called the hippocampus. The hippocampus is also part of your limbic system and is in the shape of a horseshoe. So everyone make a horseshoe shape like this:

The hippocampus is known as the librarian of the brain because it files everything processed through the senses. An individual can be born with a damaged hippocampus. However, the hippocampus can also be damaged by trauma, stress, and even disease. It is in charge of short-term memory; therefore it is the beginning of learning. Individuals who

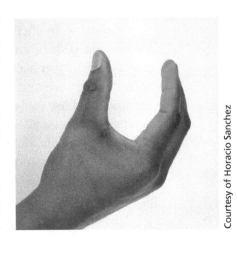

Courtesy of Horacio Sanchez

have part of the hippocampus removed can remember things prior to the surgery but cannot develop new memories. The hippocampus enables us to see the world three dimensionally. It also performs two other vital functions: flexibility (the ability to apply what has been learned to new situations) and transitive inference (the ability to infer a logical conclusion). So in many ways the hippocampus controls learning. Can we all repeat the following phrase out loud while making the gesture for the hippocampus?

The hippocampus controls learning.

Let's assign a visual to represent each of our key facts about two key parts of the limbic system:

| Two Key Parts of the Limbic Brain | |
|---|---|
| | *The amygdala controls emotions.* |
| | *The hippocampus controls learning.* |

anna1311/iStock/Thinkstock

AlexandrMoroz/iStock/Thinkstock

From now on when you see the almond symbol, I want you to make the almond gesture and say, "The amygdala controls emotions." From now on when you see the horseshoe symbol, I want you to make the horseshoe gesture and say, "The hippocampus controls learning." Once the students have reviewed the two key points enough, the teacher will remove the language and have the students recall the key points utilizing gestures or visuals alone. Over time, the teacher will also increase the speed at which the students do the recall. It is important that the teacher introduce students to three key points concerning learning. These points should not only be introduced but also be repeated with regularity.

1. All learning requires the recall of key facts.

   – You cannot write an essay about a book without recalling any of the characters or events.

2. The use of repetition, visual cues, and movements is designed to improve the brain's ability to recall things that have been learned quickly.

   – This is a more advanced way of learning that should be utilized for the rest of their lives. Help students validate the point by showing them random logos and have them recall the catch-phrase associated with each product.

3. If you can recall key points quickly, your brain will be better able to remember all the additional information you learned related to that fact.

   – This is a strategy that can help you no longer become stressed when taking a test. Merely recall key points that have been con-sistently reviewed, and then relax because your brain will help you recall additional related information.

# Learning Principles and Applications Through Embodied Cognition

## THIS CHAPTER

This chapter introduces the discovery of embodied cognition, which reveals how the brain learns abstract concepts through the human body.

Embodied cognition occurs when the brain has the body engage in a range of unconscious actions to improve comprehension of abstract concepts. The exciting finding of embodied cognition provides teachers with a blueprint about how to teach advanced concepts with greater ease.

## INTRODUCTION

Starting in the early 1970s, cognitive psychologists and linguists began to question the traditional understanding of language—a process where concepts are attached to words thereby giving the words meaning. The new movement proposed that the meaning of language was not a process by which we translate words into actual concepts. Rather, the meaning of language is a process in which cognitive definitions are given depth of understanding through subconscious and unconscious meaning provided through the human body. This movement took on the name *embodiment*. Proponents believed meaning is not distilled away from our bodily experiences but is instead intricately related. There were two distinct stages of this movement: the earlier, which was philosophical, and the latter, which was scientific.

## WHAT DOES THE RESEARCH SAY ABOUT EMBODIED COGNITION?

The early movement of embodiment was led by linguists, especially those at U.C. Berkeley including George Lakoff and others. It was not until the mid-1990s when a group of neuroscientists in Parma, Italy, began to think that the understanding of language is, in fact, a simulation in our minds. Our minds go through a process of attempting to experience the things that language describes. This sounds logical; however, prior to this point, language was thought to be a cognitive process in which the prefrontal cortex analyzes the meaning of a word and produces the connotation. Until embodiment, sensory input was viewed only as unanalyzed information routed from the body to the cortex for processing and understanding.

The overt embodiment idea was that we consciously conjure up *mental imagery* in our brain when we process language. This mental imagery produces a mental simulation. For example, the phrase, "the smell of my mom's apple pie" might bring to our conscious mind the memory of what it was like to smell apple pie baking when you were a child. However, researches began to believe that when we process language, the brain often engages in unconscious simulations of which we are completely unaware. If the brain did not engage in these unconscious simulations, much of the meaning of language would be compromised. Simply put, researchers began to note that the brain produces sights we don't consciously see, sensory experiences we are not aware we are reliving, and even movements we do not know we are making. The brain is constantly working on processes of which we are unaware in an effort to give a fuller meaning to the spoken or read word.

In 2009, Niedenthal and her colleagues conducted two studies that began to move embodied cognition from theory to reality. In the first study, she used an electromyography to measure facial muscle activity and found that while reading emotional words, subtle facial muscles unconsciously moved whenever the reader was attempting to comprehend words in a text that carried deep arousing meaning. Words such as disgust, vomit, and foul increased facial muscle activity involving the curling of the lips, wrinkling of the nose, and the furrowing of the brow. Facial activity was thought to actually simulate the common facial expression associated with emotions that were transpiring in the brain.

Niedenthal's second experiment began to crystallize just how significant facial movements are to the comprehension of language. In the second experiment, she prohibited participants' abilities to smile or frown. The results were that altering these simple movements seemed to alter the meaning of language. Language designed to produce happiness or sadness lost much of its impact when natural movements were prohibited. However, when participants were able to move their lips, the impact of similar language was restored (Niedenthal, Winkielman, Mondillon, & Vermeulen, 2009). Niedenthal has come to believe that the brain cannot fully think about emotions without engaging in some form of reenactment or physical simulation.

The impact of what happens when people's ability to simulate specific emotional expressions was further seen in a 2009 study. Neurologist Andreas Hennenlotter and his colleagues at the Munich University of Technology gave participants Botox injections to the forehead, temporarily paralyzing the muscles that are responsible for frowning. The treatment was found to mute activity in the amygdala. The amygdala plays a significant role in producing emotion and in reading emotional cues. Furthermore, the amygdala produces an automated form of mimicking expressions of others, which plays a vital role in promoting empathy. The results suggest that by preventing natural muscle response, Botox treatments jammed signals between neural circuitry, blocking the feeling associated with the emotional experience (Hennenlotter et al., 2009). The results also clearly indicated that if you alter subconscious movement, you change the very meaning of the experience. These findings were further bolstered in a 2010 study led by Glenberg when through

Botox treatment, he was able to lower comprehension of sad, angry, or happy sentences by limiting subconscious facial movements (Havas, Glenberg, Gutowski, Lucarelli, & Davidson, 2010). The flexing of our facial muscles does not merely reflect our emotions but is necessary for our ability to experience the feeling.

It should be noted that subconscious and unconscious physical responses to experiences not only shape our perception, but also determine our judgments and ultimately behaviors. Research conducted by Cannon, Schnall, and White (2011) determined through the use of electromyography that an individual's affect prior to making a moral decision is predictive of subsequent behavior. In addition, the intensity of the facial expressions correlated to the extremity of the moral judgment. In life situations such as a courtroom, these subconscious or unconscious reactions determine guilt or innocence, life or death.

## THE BRAIN'S SUBCONSCIOUS AND UNCONSCIOUS BATTLE TO BRING MEANING TO LANGUAGE

The plethora of research studies in the field of embodied cognition concluded that comprehension of language is not solely performed by the prefrontal cortex. In these research studies, subconscious and unconscious sensory and motor circuits do not merely feed signals to the cortex for comprehension; these experiences perform a level of cognition independently. Many things take place in other regions of the brain and body simultaneously that shape language comprehension. Language comprehension is altered before the cortex can form an opinion by subconscious and unconscious automated body responses. Research shows that automated body responses provide ongoing meaning to written and verbal communication. Researchers perceive these body responses as automated because viewing facial expressions triggers similar expressions on one's own face, even in the absence of conscious recognition (Preston & de Waal, 2002). Similarly, studies indicate that limiting any automated body movement lowers cognitive capacity to comprehend written or spoken language because it changes the experience.

In addition, the comprehension of language is highly influenced by subconscious and unconscious memories. Even a lost memory can influence comprehension. How is it possible that lost memories can influence thought and even behavior? Studies suggest that traces of lost memories remain in a cell's nucleus. Any experience related to a lost memory triggers cell activation. Individuals do not have memories of their first years of life. However, highly emotional unconscious infant memories are encoded in the brain's neural circuitry. These memories strongly influence comprehension when triggered. Subconscious and unconscious memories occur in milliseconds constantly to aid in comprehension. It is actually easier to reason away explicit thoughts that might influence your comprehension. However, it is impossible to defend against implicit experiences that influence comprehension.

This new understanding of linguistic expression produces new challenges. Our breadth of experiences is crucial to comprehension because it provides conscious and unconscious memories that allow the brain to produce more accurate comprehension. Students with limited exposure experience less subconscious and unconscious memories firing to provide a deeper understanding of language. Another challenge is that a segment of the population has limited subconscious and unconscious body responses to language that hamper accurate comprehension. The brain's process of triggering conscious and unconscious memories and body responses when interpreting the spoken or written language is what allows individuals to take one-dimensional words and transform them into a three-dimensional world.

One of the facts that psychologists have known for years is that individuals with limited affect seem not to be able to read the social cues of others and possess a lower level of empathy. The inability to produce subtle physical responses to the cues of others limited these individuals from experiencing a productive and happy social life. However, it is now known that the hampering of automated subconscious and unconscious physical responses inhibits more than social and emotional comprehension. The hindering of automated subconscious and unconscious physical responses severely limits the comprehension of written or verbal language as well.

Let's consider one example of how unconscious body responses help us comprehend abstract language. Time is an abstract concept: We are taught to understand it in terms of seconds, minutes, hours, days, past, and future. However, our bodies are hard at work providing unconscious aids to our comprehension. Lynden Miles and his Aberdeen colleagues Louise Nind and Neil Macrae fitted 20 participants with a motion sensor while they imagined future or past events. After just 15 seconds, participants who were recalling the past had swayed backward an average of about 0.07 inches (1.5 to 2 mm), while the future thinkers, leaned forward about 0.1 inches (3 mm) (Miles, Karpinska, Lumsden, & Macrae, 2010). We can all agree that college students possess a very sound understanding of the concept of time. However, it is likely that in the development of that understanding of the language related to time, the body made subtle movements to aid in early comprehension. What clearly indicates that the body is at work in understanding language is that the body responses change to match different interpretations of language. For example, in Aymara, an Amerindian language of the Andes, the future is described as being behind them with the past in front. Studies found that the Amerindian who speak Aymara sway backward when thinking about future events and forward when thinking about the past (Núñez & Sweetser, 2006). This is a clear indication that the body is at work unconsciously to help in language comprehension. If it were merely innate movements, they would be universal regardless of cultural understanding.

The influence of body experiences is also seen in how we express abstract concepts daily. Siri Carpenter (2008) states that the use of metaphors that join the body and mind reflect the fact our brains gain insight from our bodies to make sense of abstract concepts. Metaphors such as looking up to those we respect, stooping down to their level, thinking warmly about loved ones, hiding dirty secrets, feeling the weight being lifted off our shoulders, and looking back on the past and forward to the future are all examples of how the body aids the mind in comprehension of abstract concepts. These internal aids naturally developed into common expressions because they are so widely experienced.

## EMBODIED COGNITION STRATEGIES

A teacher can accomplish two things by incorporating embodied cognition strategies. First, embodied cognition strategies increase comprehension of abstract concepts. Second, the teacher can aid students who do not produce a sufficient amount of automated body responses to experience embodied cognition to improve the depth of their understanding.

Embodied cognition strategies include visuals, movements, rhythmic patterns, touch, and even taste. Sometimes recalling an emotional experience can change our heart rate, facial expressions, and body posture. Thus, what the body experiences can change what we think. Research has shown that we all begin as visual learners. The brain automatically goes through a visual simulation process whenever we touch, hear, or smell something, and the process exists even if sight is not present. For the majority of the world, comprehending as an infant is based on what we see and associating the images with language and emotions. Traditionally visual learning has had two well-accepted processes. The first is that visual stimuli are assigned labels and values that are commonly accepted and known either across the globe or regionally. The second is that visual stimuli are associated with life experiences and are often assigned emotional values. The outcomes of these two processes are that most individuals within a certain region are exposed to common visual stimuli and often have shared experiences.

It is both learned labels and shared experiences that provide an age-appropriate comprehension of language. The reality is that most teachers have subconscious or even conscious assumptions concerning what most students at certain grade levels should know based merely on the persistent exposure to hundreds of students. This assumption is often the platform from where teaching begins. However, some students have not had the same level of exposure and are unable to label certain visual stimuli. They also are void of personal experiences that give visual stimuli meaning. For example, a teacher says, "A blue wildebeest grazed on the planes of the Serengeti." A person with a visual knowledge of a blue wildebeest and the Serengeti could begin to assign a value to the language. If the student has any level of personal experience, such as seeing a documentary, reading about Africa, or even visiting the Serengeti, he or she would be able to have some context—the Serengeti is a geographical region in Africa that is home to a diverse number of large mammals including gazelles, zebras, buffalo, and blue wildebeests. The student can likely produce very similar images as depicted below in his or her mind.

Fuse/iStock/Thinkstock

Gim42/iStock/Thinkstock

However, a student with no visual understanding of the term blue wildebeests or the Serengeti might have to guess based on what past knowledge he or she has had. Focusing on the words that the student has comprehension of—blue and beast, he or she might imagine what is depicted below:

mychadre77/iStock/Thinkstock

The goal of embodied cognition is to utilize experiences that incorporate the senses or movement to assist the brain in developing a deeper understanding of more advanced concepts. Another way to phrase this is to help students reach an understanding at a chemical level. Teachers have been developing experiences that enhance learning since the inception of formal instruction! A simple way to begin to comprehend embodied cognition is merely to analyze activities that you as a teacher have conducted that successfully aided students in learning advanced concepts more readily. In dissecting these activities, teachers will be able to tease out sensory elements that were triggered, producing a form of embodied cognition.

A teacher is introducing her elementary class to the concept of syllables. To aid in their comprehension, the teacher will utilize movements. She tells students that a syllable is a part of a word and all words are made up of one or more syllables. Then she tells them that she knows a trick so they can always know how many syllables are in a word. First, she has each student place the top of their right hand directly under their chin. She informs them that every time they say a syllable their mouths have to open and close. Therefore, each time their hand moves they have said a syllable. Then they practice. After the students have understood the concept, the teacher has them hold up their left hand in a fist, and each time their right hand moves under their chin when they say a word, they should raise a finger from their left fist representing each syllable. For example, if the word is robot, their right hand under their chin will move two times so they should hold up two fingers on their left hand. This way the teacher can go through a list of words and see how well the students are doing. Once the students seem to accurately feel syllables by the movement of their hands, the teacher can transition to how well students hear syllables by teaching them to clap for every syllable they hear in a word that she says. For example, if she says "basketball," they should all clap three times.

A history teacher conducting a lesson of the Egyptian pyramids might utilize a video of the pyramids to provide a visual of the breadth and scope of the pyramids when discussing their construction. The visual representation will clearly illustrate the size of each stone and allow students to see the pyramids in relation to a person, driving home the point of why they are considered one of the Seven Wonders of the World. Reading a description of the dimensions of the pyramids will lead to only a limited comprehension of language for any student lacking sufficient related knowledge. However, watching someone describe the construction while showing how each stone was set in place allows the brain to apply the full range of analyses that occurs whenever we judge what we see.

In the discovery of DNA, Watson and Crick believed that each strand of the DNA molecule was a template for the other. The new theory was that during cell division the two strands separate and on each strand a new "other half" is built, just like the one before. However, it was not until they built the structure with their own hands and it so perfectly fit the experimental data that it was almost immediately accepted. DNA's discovery has been called the most important biological work of the last 100 years. Watson identified touch as playing a crucial role in the comprehension of the missing pieces in the uncovering of DNA. Touch allowed the brains of these experts to do calculations subconsciously and fill in missing gaps.

The above-mentioned illustrations are a few examples of embodied cognition. If our brains' are wired to learn in this fashion, isn't it incumbent on educators to begin to apply movement, visuals, touch, smell, and even taste to the learning experience? The most encouraging aspect of embodied cognition is that it advances comprehension from a basic to a more advanced level. When teachers apply embodied cognition strategies, they not only help students who lack related knowledge, but they also allow students with advanced understandings to make more meaningful gains.

# The Goal of Higher-Level Thinking

Rawpixel Ltd/iStock/Thinkstock

## THIS CHAPTER

Recent neuroscientific findings on how higher-level thinking occurs dispel earlier-held myths. The studies indicate that higher-ordered thinking is more a product of how we learn rather than cognitive ability. The encouraging news is that teachers can increase the occurrence of higher-ordered thinking by increasing automation of core information and promoting long-term potentiation through embodied cognition. This chapter also addresses a surprising finding that reveals a strong correlation between healthy social behavior and increased activity in the regions of the brain primarily responsible for higher-level thinking.

## WHAT IS HIGHER-LEVEL THINKING?

*Higher-level thinking* is simply defined as the brain making connections, which allows students to link new information to old and draw unique conclusions based on their prior knowledge. Synaptic connections increase in a few ways. One way is sleep, which is why many people go to bed thinking about a problem and wake up with the solution. The brain makes sophisticated connections that produce higher-level thinking during REM sleep. Individuals who are born with a difficult or shy and anxious temperament will naturally struggle with sleep, and the busy lifestyle of the 21st century has contributed to higher numbers of individuals struggling with poor sleeping habits. Stress and poor eating habits can also cause sleep issues. It is safe to say that a significant portion of the student population is not getting enough sleep, which can definitely hamper higher-level thinking.

In addition, the depth of prior knowledge determines the ease with which one can make connections to previous learning. The depth of understanding on any topic determines the density of connections in the brain reflecting the quality of synaptic networks. In addition, the depth of understanding on a topic improves the ease of connections to a wider breadth of knowledge, increasing the odds that new associations will be made. These connected networks are why a student's excelling in any area increases the potential for future learning.

## EXERCISE

Individuals who exercise on a consistent basis can experience an increase in higher-level thinking skills. Many people find that they have solved a problem that they were pondering or reached a level of deeper clarity after engaging in exercise. Exercise activates many of the regions of the brain responsible for increasing synaptic connections. Part of the reason exercise enhances cognition is that it increases blood flow. When blood flow increases, it produces more energy and oxygen to the brain, enhancing performance. Also, the hippocampus, which is highly involved in learning and memory, increases activity during exercise.

Research shows that when activity increases in the hippocampus, cognitive function improves. For example, when mice run, it improves their spatial learning (Creer, Romberg, Saksida, van Praag, & Bussey, 2010). Another study demonstrated that increasing aerobic exercise can actually reverse hippocampal damage (Erickson et al., 2009). This means exercise can improve the shrinkage of the hippocampus that often occurs from abuse or with aging (Teicher, Samson, Polcari, & McGreenery, 2006). In addition, another study found that students who consistently exercised performed better on tests than their sedentary peers (Castelli, Hillman, & Buck, 2007).

## HOW TEACHERS CAN INCREASE HIGHER-LEVEL THINKING

Teachers often focus on producing higher-level thinking through traditional instruction. While teachers may recognize when higher-level thinking occurs with individual students, they don't necessarily know how to consciously increase its occurrence. The process of learning does spur on higher-level thinking but does not necessarily guarantee that it will happen. Therefore, many teachers often perceive that certain students get it and others do not. Even more tragic is the fact that some educators believe that higher-level thinking is a level of understanding that is reserved for the more intellectually gifted students. *Science has dispelled the notion that higher-level thinking is correlated with intellect.* The truth is that higher-level thinking is a natural occurrence of the human brain. It is the brain making connections to prior knowledge producing deeper levels of comprehension.

What methods of instruction increase the occurrence of higher-level thinking to boost its production? The first crucial requirement for higher-level thinking is automation. Higher-level thinking requires that fundamental knowledge be retrieved quickly. With each repetition, the brain does not have to expend such high energy recognizing, comprehending, and recalling. Automation allows for other cognitive processes to occur, creating more advanced associations (Buckner, Raichle, Miezin, & Petersen, 1996).

Bloom conducted a 5-year study of geniuses in six fields: concert pianists, sculptors, tennis stars, Olympic swimmers, research mathematicians, and research neurologists. He made a direct link between their advanced achievements and the hours spent on gaining automation of key related knowledge (Bloom, 1985). The study noted that all the geniuses practiced an average of 25 to 50 hours a week for 12 to 16 years to obtain the pinnacle in their perspective fields. The conclusion reached was that only at a level of automaticity can the brain make profound connections.

The same conclusion reached by Bloom was further supported by two other studies related to higher-level thinking. Researchers concluded that the clearest index of automaticity is that other conscious cognitive processes take place simultaneously (Bahrick & Shelly, 1958; LaBerge & Samuels, 1974). In other words, one of the best indicators that higher-level thinking will be achieved is the automation of key fundamental knowledge.

Brain research conducted by Just and Keller (2009) studied students receiving 6 months of intensive remedial reading instruction. The study showed that repetition by poor readers not only improved their reading skills, but also grew new white matter, fatty myelin sheaths that encase the nerve fibers and connect one "thinking" area of the brain with another. White matter pathways play a crucial role in helping the brain perform complex cognitive tasks more efficiently. The most surprising finding was that white matter gains had more to do with the frequency of practice rather than how skilled people were becoming on a given task.

The human brain is designed to be transformed based on how often we engage in certain tasks. Since the brain learns only a portion of what is presented daily, actions that are repeated are prioritized for short-term memory. The brain protects the things we do the most with myelin sheaths that increase the rate of recall and the likelihood that the information will make connections with prior knowledge. Over time, repetition becomes the low-energy-consuming foundation that allows the brain to focus its limited resources on more advanced connections.

The take-home message is that the road to higher-level thinking begins with the automation of the foundational elements of the subject matter. Teachers don't always identify core areas, which means that students won't learn them to the point of automation. The more someone continues to concentrate in any area of learning, the larger the body of information that reaches a level of automation. Even though academic standards place an emphasis on higher-level thinking, we must ensure that students develop a sufficient level of automation related to advanced learning content.

The second crucial requirement for higher-level thinking is embodied cognition. Whenever the brain is primed naturally or artificially through applied teaching strategies with an embodied cognition experience, it seems to create a place for new learning concepts. For example, in a recent study, students were shown a picture related to a story that they were about to read. Brain scans identified that this simple action stimulates the posterior retrosplenial cortex (PRC) to improve recall while students are reading (Rudge & Warrington, 1991; Valenstein et al., 1987). The stimulation of the PRC also lowered distractibility (Fletcher et al., 1995). In addition, seeing a visual cue related to the story, prior to reading, activates the medial parietal/posterior cingulate cortex, which increases comprehension. Later studies concluded that embodied cognition experiences provide a mental framework that enables new information to be easily stored (Bransford, 1979; Johnson-Laird, 1983; Van Dijk & Kintsch, 1983).

The learning process is fickle. When individuals are introduced to information that they can easily understand, the brain requires very little energy and experiences a low level of chemical disturbance. However, when new learning is not understood, it generates a level of chemical activity that hinders the learning process. Students who suffer from any form of emotional disorder or are exposed to consistent stress often experience a chemical surge in the brain that is unconsciously irritating. The irritating chemical experience can result in the avoidance of more challenging information in the future. The encouraging news is that embodied cognition experiences seem to lower the brain's chemical reaction to new learning by priming the brain to receive and better comprehend new information. The result is a better learning experience that is not irritable and, therefore, avoided.

Memories that can be recalled quickly are better able to link to incoming information to aid in retention and comprehension. When a well-developed body of implicit knowledge exists, it begins to generate understanding and even create abstract concepts (when introduced or independently obtained). A brain possessing a wealth of related facts that has an understanding of a range of related concepts begins to produce more advanced thoughts, often referred to as *higher-level thinking*.

When automated core information and principles learned through embodied cognition come together, students suddenly see the scope of learning and begin to connect it to a breadth of related and even unrelated prior learning. They can draw conclusions and ask relevant questions. Students engaging in higher-level thinking have been captured through functional magnetic resonance imaging (fMRI). Cohen's (2008) team found that the area known as the ventromedial orbitofrontal cortex is activated when there is sufficient automation and embodied cognition, which produces increased blood flow activity in this region resulting in increased comprehension.

## HIGHER-LEVEL THINKING AND SOCIAL INTERACTION

The researchers found that the more students experienced higher-level thinking, the more they sought new learning experiences. In addition, higher-level learning experiences create stronger connections between certain regions of the brain. The brain regions involved in decision making, the hippocampus and amygdala, become more strongly linked to the area involved in emotion and reward, the ventral and mesial striatum. The improved connection to the ventral and mesial striatum transforms the process of higher-level thinking into a rewarding experience. Once higher-level thinking is rewarded, it creates a desire for additional higher-level thinking experiences. The most shocking finding is that individuals who desire to get along with others had stronger than normal connections between the striatum and the prefrontal cortex. Researchers believe that there is a strong correlation between socialization and higher-ordered thinking.

The role social interaction plays in learning should not be surprising. Research clearly indicates that children require a social setting and social interaction with other human beings to activate the brain's ability to learn a language (Kuhl, 2011). The theory that social factors are the gateway to learning may explain not only how children typically acquire language, but also why children with autism often exhibit deficits in social cognition and language (Kuhl, Coffey-Corina, Padden, & Dawson, 2005). Neuroscience has provided concrete support to the hypothesis that social factors play a far more significant role than previously realized in human learning across domains throughout our lifetimes (Meltzoff, Kuhl, Movellan, & Sejnowski, 2009).

If social approval plays such a vital role in higher-ordered thinking, then how does one explain very intelligent students on the autism spectrum? The answer to that question is pretty straightforward. The human brain is designed to compensate for inherent deficits. A common finding is that if an individual loses his or her eyesight, then the capacities of the other senses become heightened. Intelligent students on the autism spectrum experience a very similar compensation. Individuals with savant syndrome, the ability to demonstrate profound abilities in one area, often suffer from neurodevelopmental disorders or brain injuries.

## AN EXAMPLE OF HOW
## HIGHER-LEVEL THINKING OCCURS

*A child is introduced to fairy tale stories early in life. Her parents read them to her each evening. She has a favorite story that she asks her parents to read as the last story each night. She merely has to see the picture on the page, and she knows exactly what will happen. Eventually, she can recite the story from memory. As the young girl begins to read, she continues to be drawn to fairy tales. Over the course of her short life, she has heard hundreds of fairy tales, has read over 50 to herself, watched Disney movies depicting her favorite tales repeatedly, and committed a few books to memory. She has become an expert on fairy tale stories. She even acts out scenes from her favorite stories, playing the parts of each character.*

*The young girl loves her fairy tales so much that while she reads, her parents can tell when the hero of the story is in trouble by the look on their daughter's face. The stories sometimes bring her to tears, but in the end always make her happy. One day, the young girl tells her mother that she no longer fears for the heroes in her tales because she notices that the books seem to always begin with "once upon a time" and end with "and they lived happily ever after." She can even predict what will happen next in every new fairy tale she reads. She now knows that there is always a hero and a villain. Although things will always look tragic for the hero, in the end good will triumph over evil.*

*One day her father brings her a different kind of story; he calls it a tragedy. She reads the story and immediately notices that in fairy tales the good guy always wins, but in the tragedy the good guy does not win. She asks her father if all tragedies end with the hero suffering. Her father says yes, that is why they call it a tragedy. That evening the little girl begins to wonder—are fairy tales true or is life more like a tragedy? The next day at school, her teacher has the students write a short story. The little girl immediately knows what she will do; she will write a fairy tale that looks like a tragedy until, at the last moment, the hero wins.*

This simple example illustrates the natural occurrence of the three elements of learning. In the initial stage, the young girl was introduced to something new, a fairy tale. It was through repetition, countless visuals, imagination, and even role-play that she memorized stories. Most of the foundations of a fairy tale became automated knowledge that she could easily recognize and eventually predict. This level of understanding led her to recognize patterns and concepts. The emotional response to the story is evidence that embodied cognition was naturally occurring in her brain. It is likely that the young girl experienced many of the emotions the author intended, as indicated by her facial twitches associated with emotional words providing a deeper level of comprehension. Her experience while reading represents the highest level of embodied cognition—empathy. These embodied cognition experiences eventually produced more than just awareness of patterns and concepts but led to higher-ordered thinking. When introduced to a new genre of literature, the young girl could quickly demonstrate forms of higher-level thinking. She was able to compare and contrast because her knowledge of fairy tales was so automated. In addition, embodied cognition experiences helped her learn advanced concepts that became so well understood that her brain was free to perform higher-ordered thinking. In the end, the girl managed very advanced forms of higher-level thinking, the constructing of complex questions, and the ability to create her own fairy tale independently based on prior knowledge.

This example represents the natural occurrence of higher-ordered thinking. However, individuals placed at risk by life's circumstances often are not exposed to an adequate level of repetition and do not produce sufficient internal embodied cognition experiences. For these individuals, deeper meaning is lost unless teachers incorporate an adequate amount of repetition and utilize embodied cognition strategies when introducing advanced concepts. When these two steps are taken, higher-ordered thinking is merely a natural occurrence of the human brain. It is simply the brain making connections. For a sample lesson describing how teachers can establish higher-level thinking skills in a class with children at different levels, refer to the supplement model lesson on the next page.

# CHAPTER 6 SUPPLEMENT MODEL LESSON

dolgachov/iStock/Thinkstock

**A**s we have established, higher-level thinking is literally the brain making connections. Teachers can promote higher-level thinking by utilizing activities that force the brain to make desired connections without spoon-feeding students solutions. Think of instruction in terms of a jigsaw puzzle. The core information is the border pieces that provide a frame to help better solve the puzzle. The very distinct objects in the puzzle are the principles and applications taught through embodied cognition. These are often easier to see and assemble. Higher-level thinking is the remaining pieces that are more nebulous. These puzzle pieces would be impossible to put in place unless all the prior work had transpired. This is why teachers should create activities after automating core information and promoting concepts through embodied cognition that lead students to assemble the essential components learned and arrive at higher-ordered conclusions on their own. Higher-ordered thinking is, in fact, the evidence that the instruction has taken hold. It is the teacher's gauge that he or she has done a successful job of imparting information. A specific example of a higher-level thinking activity is provided in this chapter.

The following model lesson is based directly on the fifth-grade Standard Course of Study.

## VOCABULARY ACQUISITION AND USE

- CCSS.ELA-Literacy.L.5.5 Demonstrate understanding of figurative language, word relationships, and nuances in word meanings.
  - CCSS.ELA-Literacy.L.5.5a Interpret figurative language, including similes and metaphors, in context.
  - CCSS.ELA-Literacy.L.5.5b Recognize and explain the meaning of common idioms, adages, and proverbs.
  - CCSS.ELA-Literacy.L.5.5c Use the relationship between particular words (e.g., synonyms, antonyms, homographs) to understand each of the words better.

Imagine you have inherited a fifth-grade class where a number of students have missed learning blocks related to figurative language. In the third grade, students were to have learned terms related to figurative language and their meanings, and they were to begin exploring the concept of literal versus nonliteral meaning in literature. In the fourth grade, students should have learned many of the words and meanings used in defining figurative language. Students should have had an in-depth learning experience related to similes and metaphors from which fifth-grade teachers could begin to teach the advanced material contained in the fifth-grade Standard Course of Study.

Teachers are now left to wonder if they can teach the information in the fifth-grade standards without losing the students who are missing the most basic foundations, while still challenging the advanced students in their class. The higher-level thinking goals that are designed to be the culmination of a 3-year process seem unobtainable for a number of students in the class.

Understanding the three levels of learning will allow a teacher to look at the overwhelming dilemma of reaching advanced learning goals by breaking the curriculum down into manageable segments. Addressing each level of learning improves the probability that students with a range of deficits will attain some level of the higher-ordered thinking goals. First, the teacher has to identify the minimal required core information. In this case, the core information is the terms and definitions of figurative language that should have been learned in third grade. The goal is to get this information to the level of automation by the end of the series on figurative language. The teacher calculates that 5 days will be spent on figurative language. How to structure the automation of terms related to figurative language and their meanings are described in the following paragraphs.

At the beginning and end of the English period, the students will review the chart provided. Each review should take no more than a few minutes. The chart attempts to group brain-based learning strategies that are designed to increase the rate of recall and retention more efficiently. The chart assigns each figurative language term a visual cue. The symbols help students be able pictorially to recall a cue that will help bring back related language. Next, the chart reduces the definitions to catchphrases. Remember, the hippocampus, which is in charge of short-term memory, is not attracted to large chunks of language. The chart also provides an example of each figurative language term covered in the standards. The example provided is directly correlated to the visual cue so that if the student can remember the visual, it will be easy to recall the example. The teacher will also introduce a tempo that the students will utilize when reciting elements in the chart. The tempo provides a rhythm to learning that offers an additional strategy to aid in recall. Over time, this tempo will also be increased to improve myelination (the fatty sheaths that encase the nerve fibers to make recall more efficient).

| Figurative Language | | |
|---|---|---|
| **Term** | **Definition** | **Example** |
| **Simile** | Compares using "like" or "as" | *Busy <u>as</u> a bee.* |
| **Metaphor** | Compares without using like or as | *You are what you eat.* |
| **Personification** | Human characteristics to animal or object | *My teddy bear takes a bubble bath.* |

| Term | Definition | Example |
|------|------------|---------|
| **Alliteration** | Repeats initial letter or sound | *She sells seashells by the seashore.* |
| **Onomatopoeia** | Imitates natural sounds | *Snap, crackle, pop* |
| **Hyperbole** | Exaggerates | *Pancakes a mile high* |

From top: aleksandr-mansurov-ru/iStock/Thinkstock; bod_stock/iStock/Thinkstock; AlinaMaksimova/iStock/Thinkstock; Nicolaiivanovici/iStock/Thinkstock; olegtoka/iStock/Thinkstock; dkgilbey/iStock/Thinkstock

On Day 3 the teacher will make two adjustments to the review process. The teacher will remove the example, forcing the students to recall it using only the visual cue and definition. Also, the teacher will inform the students that the tempo for reciting the chart will be faster because that will help them remember more efficiently.

| Figurative Language | | |
|------|------------|---------|
| **Term** | **Definition** | **Example** |
| **Simile** | Compares using "like" or "as" | |
| **Metaphor** | Compares without using like or as | |

| Term | Definition | Example |
|------|-----------|---------|
| **Personification** | Human characteristics to animal or object | |
| **Alliteration** | Repeats initial letter or sound | |
| **Onomatopoeia** | Imitates natural sounds | |
| **Hyperbole** | Exaggerates | |

From top: aleksandr-mansurov-ru/iStock/Thinkstock; bod_stock/iStock/Thinkstock; AlinaMaksimova/iStock/Thinkstock; Nicolaiivanovici/iStock/Thinkstock; olegtoka/iStock/Thinkstock; dkgilbey/iStock/Thinkstock

On Day 4 the teacher will eliminate the definitions, forcing the students to recall another aspect of the chart using only the visual cue and the example. The teacher will again increase the tempo.

| Figurative Language | | |
|------|-----------|---------|
| **Term** | **Definition** | **Example** |
| **Simile** | | *Busy <u>as</u> a bee.* |

| Term | Definition | Example |
|------|------------|---------|
| **Metaphor** | | *You are what you eat.* |
| **Personification** | | *My teddy bear takes a bubble bath.* |
| **Alliteration** | | *She sells seashells by the seashore.* |
| **Onomatopoeia** | | *Snap, crackle, pop* |
| **Hyperbole** | | *Pancakes a mile high* |

From top: aleksandr-mansurov-ru/iStock/Thinkstock; bod_stock/iStock/Thinkstock; AlinaMaksimova/iStock/Thinkstock; Nicolaiivanovici/iStock/Thinkstock; olegtoka/iStock/Thinkstock; dkgilbey/iStock/Thinkstock

On Day 5 the teacher removes the definitions and the example and has the students recite the chart using only the visual cue. That means whenever students do figurative language in the future, all they have to do is remember the picture to bring back the definitions and the examples. Then have the students repeat the chart, first at a slow rate of speed, then faster, and faster, until they have exhausted their limits. It is clear that this approach meets all the rules for achieving long-term potentiation because it provided repetition, reduced language, and brain-based strategies.

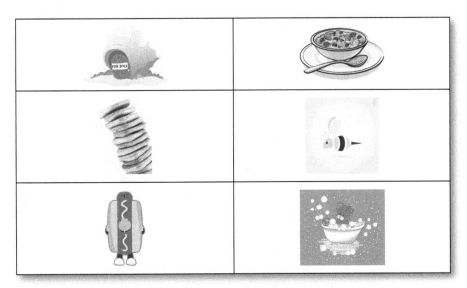

From top: aleksandr-mansurov-ru/iStock/Thinkstock; bod_stock/iStock/Thinkstock; AlinaMaksimova/iStock/Thinkstock; Nicolaiivanovici/iStock/Thinkstock; olegtoka/iStock/Thinkstock; dkgilbey/iStock/Thinkstock

The second step is to identify principles and applications in the standards. From the first day of teaching figurative language, the teacher begins to teach concepts related to each example of figurative language with the goal of increasing students comfort not only with recognizing different forms but in utilizing them as well. This is where the teacher applies strategies related to embodied cognition. See the example provided below.

The teacher shows the class the following picture and asks them what figurative language they will be covering today in class.

dkgilbey/iStock/Thinkstock

## HYPERBOLE

The teacher asks, "What is the definition of hyperbole?" and the students all say, "Big exaggeration." The teacher then introduces a gesture that the class will do every time they say the word hyperbole. Students will make their hands go from the narrow position to the wide position (see picture below that symbolizes the gesture). The teacher is utilizing a movement to help

VectorSilhouettes/iStock/Thinkstock

the brain associate the concept of a big exaggeration (an embodied cognition strategy to help internalize a concept).

## Big Exaggeration

The teacher then introduces a rhythmic pattern to the class. The teacher says, "Hyperbole man, that's like a million times harder!" Then the class says, "Take something true, and then exaggerate it way further." The chant is a rhythmic pattern that further enhances the definition of what a hyperbole is and might be utilized by those students whose brains recall rhythms better than visuals or gestures. After the class has practiced this rhythmic chant, the teacher introduces a game. The teacher tells the class that she will say the first half of the chant, the students will say the second half, and then the teacher will select a student and say a phrase. The student in turn will have to change the phrase into a hyperbole. After the process has been repeated, the teacher will pick up the tempo of the chant. See example below:

**GAME TIME**    *I say,*
Hyperbole man, that's like a million times harder!

*You all say,*
Take something true, and then exaggerate it way further.

*Then I will give you something true, and you turn it into a hyperbole.*

*Example: It rained so hard last night.*
*Complete: It rained so hard my house got dented.*

Hyperbole man, that's like a million times harder!
Take something true, and then exaggerate it way further (Rhythm & Rhyme, 2015).
*Note:* Rhythm & Rhyme is an online site that can be updated by the public. It can be found here: http://genius.com/Rhythm-rhyme-results-figurative-language-lyrics

*That car is fast.*

Hyperbole man, that's like a million times harder!
Take something true, and then exaggerate it way further.
*That house is big.*

Hyperbole man, that's like a million times harder!
Take something true, and then exaggerate it way further.
*I got a lot of candy on Halloween.*

**Faster**

Hyperbole man, that's like a million times harder!
Take something true, and then exaggerate it way further.
*That girl is tall.*

Hyperbole man, that's like a million times harder!
Take something true, and then exaggerate it way further.
*That man is old.*

Hyperbole man, that's like a million times harder!
Take something true, and then exaggerate it way further.
*That sound was loud.*

Hyperbole man, that's like a million times harder!
Take something true, and then exaggerate it way further.
*Her nose is long.*

Hyperbole man, that's like a million times harder!
Take something true, and then exaggerate it way further.
*He just won some money.*

This exercise allowed the students to demonstrate immediate recall of the term and definition of the figurative language from a visual cue rather than words. A gesture was implemented to aid the brain in achieving embodied cognition. Students expand their hands to illustrate the concept of exaggeration. The rhythmic pattern was used to drive home the definition of hyperbole. The game let students practice both recognition and application of hyperbole. The game also was done in a manner that provided repetition and increased speed. Below are other examples of figurative language taught implementing the same approach.

The teacher shows the class one of the pictures and asks them what figurative language they will cover. The teacher does two forms of figurative language each day, culminating with a higher-level thinking activity on Day 5. The foundational core information is becoming automated while students are being exposed to more advanced concepts.

The teacher asks, "What is the definition of alliteration?" The class says, "Repeats initial letters and sounds." The teacher now introduces a gesture that the class will do every time they say the word alliteration. Students will point their index fingers in the air and spin it around to make the gesture for alliteration. The teacher is utilizing a movement to help the brain associate the concept of repeating letters and sounds.

**GAME TIME**   Gesture for Alliteration

Repeats

*I say,*
It's called alliteration; that's what occurs

*You all say,*
When you get the same sound at the start of every word.

*Then I give you a start*
*Start: Ben bikes*
*Complete: before breakfast and to the bookstore.*

It's called alliteration; that's what occurs
When you get the same sound at the start of every word (Rhythm & Rhyme, 2015).
*Start: Henry hikes*
*Complete:*

It's called alliteration; that's what occurs
When you get the same sound at the start of every word.
*Start: Avery awakes*
*Complete:*

It's called alliteration; that's what occurs
When you get the same sound at the start of every word.
*Start: Robert runs*
*Complete:*

**Faster**

It's called alliteration; that's what occurs
When you get the same sound at the start of every word.
*Start: Sally sells*
*Complete:*

It's called alliteration; that's what occurs
When you get the same sound at the start of every word.
*Start: Roger Rabbit*
*Complete:*

It's called alliteration; that's what occurs
When you get the same sound at the start of every word.
*Start: Lucy loves*
*Complete:*

**GAME TIME**    Gesture for Simile

Courtesy of Horacio Sanchez

Compares
*I say,*
A simile is something that you use to compare

*You all say,*
Two unrelated things with an element that's shared.

*Then I start*
*Start: Hungry*
*Complete: as a bear*

A simile is something that you use to compare
Two unrelated things with an element that's shared (Rhythm & Rhyme, 2015).
*Start: Quick*
*Complete:*

*(Continued)*

(Continued)

A simile is something that you use to compare
Two unrelated things with an element that's shared.
*Start: Mean*
*Complete:*

A simile is something that you use to compare
Two unrelated things with an element that's shared.
*Start: Quiet*
*Complete:*

**Faster**

A simile is something that you use to compare
Two unrelated things with an element that's shared.
*Start: Strong*
*Complete:*

A simile is something that you use to compare
Two unrelated things with an element that's shared.
*Start: Smells*
*Complete:*

A simile is something that you use to compare
Two unrelated things with an element that's shared.
*Start: Smart*
*Complete:*

By the fifth day, students' recall of figurative language terms, definitions, and examples have become automated enough to be triggered by merely a visual cue. Students have become comfortable with identifying and producing different forms of figurative language independently. The requirements of automation of core information and embodiment of principles and applications have been met. It is time to test students' comprehension through higher-level thinking activities.

Students are seated in groups at each table. The groups can range in size from three to six. The smaller the group, the more challenging the higher-level thinking activity will be. There are three tables in the front of the room.

- One table has cards with the symbols that the students have learned corresponding to each type of figurative language.
- The second table has the cards containing all the definitions of different types of figurative language.
- The third table has examples of figurative language but does not use any of the examples that the students have learned during the week.

Inform students that the team at each table is competing with the other tables to complete a chart like the one they used all week: creating a column of visuals, definitions, and examples. Teams will complete their assignment as fast and as accurately as possible. The team that finishes first with all the answers correct will win a bonus playing card. (So keep on working even if a team says they are done because they might not have gotten every answer correct.) When each team is done, the chart will be graded and one playing card given for each correct answer. After each team has won the number of cards earned, they will add the value of the cards. The team with the highest number of points wins. Each member of the winning team will receive a prize.

 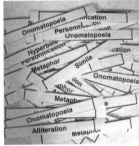 

Courtesy of Horacio Sanchez

Match the correct heading with the correct definitions and example.

- Headings are in black.
- Definitions are in blue.
- Examples are in green.
- One playing card for each correct grouping.

  - Add the value of card, the team with the most points wins
  - Winning team gets prizes.

- One representative from each table will be given an answer key and will grade another table.

| Symbol | Term | Definition | Examples |
|---|---|---|---|
| | **Simile** | A figure of speech comparing two unlike things that is often introduced by like or as. | • Busy as a bee<br>• Clean as a whistle<br>• Brave as a lion<br>• Stand out like a sore thumb<br>• As easy as shooting fish in a barrel<br>• As dry as a bone |
| | **Metaphor** | Comparing two things by using one kind of object or using in place of another to suggest the likeness between them. | • The world is my oyster.<br>• You are a couch potato.<br>• Time is money.<br>• He has a heart of stone.<br>• America is a melting pot.<br>• You are my sunshine. |
| | **Personification** | Giving something human qualities. | • Opportunity knocked on the door.<br>• The sun greeted me this morning.<br>• The sky was full of dancing stars.<br>• The vines wove their fingers together to form a braid.<br>• The radio stopped singing and stared at me.<br>• The sun played hide and seek with the clouds. |

| | Term | Definition | Examples |
|---|---|---|---|
| | **Alliteration** | The repetition of usually initial consonant sounds in two or more neighboring words or syllables. | • Alice's aunt ate apples and acorns around August.<br>• Becky's beagle barked and bayed, becoming bothersome for Billy.<br>• Carrie's cat clawed her couch, creating chaos.<br>• Dan's dog dove deep in the dam, drinking dirty water as he dove.<br>• Eric's eagle eats eggs, enjoying each episode of eating.<br>• Fred's friends fried Fritos for Friday's food. |
| | **Onomatopoeia** | Naming a thing or an action by imitating the sound associated with it. | • Is the hum of the bees<br>• The pop of a balloon<br>• The tweet of a bird<br>• Knock-knock, who's there?<br>• Baa, baa, black sheep, have you any wool?<br>• Splish-splash downhill |
| | **Hyperbole** | A big exaggeration, usually with humor | • You snore louder than a freight train.<br>• It's a slow burg, I spent a couple of weeks there one day.<br>• I had to walk 15 miles to school in the snow, uphill.<br>• You could have knocked me over with a feather.<br>• Bill Gates has enough money to feed an entire continent. |

From top: aleksandr-mansurov-ru/iStock/Thinkstock; bod_stock/iStock/Thinkstock; AlinaMaksimova/iStock/Thinkstock; Nicolaiivanovici/iStock/Thinkstock; olegtoka/iStock/Thinkstock; dkgilbey/iStock/Thinkstock

Immediately after the game has ended, transition the students into another challenge. Assemble books on three tables in the back of the class.

- One table has books for poor readers.
- One table has books for average readers.
- One table has books for advanced readers.

Assign students based on reading ability to one of the three tables. Then issue the challenge:

- From the books assembled, select one and take it to your desk. As quickly as possible begin to read through the book.
  - Identify as many examples of figurative language within the time allowed.
  - Accurately label each form of figurative language you find.
  - Write down each example you have identified next to the correct label.
  - The highest number of correct examples will win a prize at the beginning of tomorrow's English class.

The teacher can modify this exercise further to incorporate additional past learning. See example below:

- Use your knowledge of different types of literature and how books are cataloged in the library. Attempt to identify a book that will likely contain many examples of figurative language.
  - Identify the type of literature selected.

    o Provide reasons why you selected the book.

  - Then identify as many examples of figurative language as you can within the time allowed.
  - Label each example found (make sure to reference the page where the example was found).
  - Write down the definition of each type of figurative language you find.

The above activities provide examples of how higher-level thinking activities can motivate students to connect all elements of prior learning to achieve more advanced goals. In the first exercise, students had to recognize the symbol of each form of figurative language and pair it correctly with the correct definition and example. The activity was done in a competitive format to test the speed of retention.

The second activity had students utilize the same knowledge as the first activity, but this time while pairing it with reading. The activity clearly illustrates how differentiating instruction (providing books for a range of reading levels) can have all students demonstrate the identical higher-level thinking skills. All students regardless of reading ability would be able to participate and demonstrate higher-ordered thinking.

The third example illustrates how high-level activities can combine past learning with new learning to further challenge students. In this activity, the students' knowledge of different forms of literature aids in selecting a book that is likely to have more examples of figurative language. The ability to select a book that has good examples of figurative language is an indicator that the student learned the core information, principles, and applications and demonstrates higher-level thinking objectives related to different forms of literature. Those skills are then combined with core information, concepts, and higher-level thinking skills related to the mastery of figurative language. The outcomes are a range of connections that allow students to demonstrate that they are making advanced connections.

# Promoting Success Is Key to Restoring Student Motivation

Ingram Publishing/Thinkstock

## THIS CHAPTER

It is often said that we learn more from our mistakes. However, recent neuroscientific findings challenge this belief. The reality is that the only people who can learn from mistakes and failures are those who consistently experience success. This chapter explains how success is intricately linked to motivation.

## INTRODUCTION

Until this point, the focus has been on improving instruction to promote academic success for all students. However, one of the truths about the human brain is that regions do not operate in isolation. In other words, the condition and functioning of other regions can directly or indirectly impact unrelated areas of the brain. This is why academic success is not merely dependent on instruction, but also on how we nurture the whole student. In this day and age, teachers must become versed in understanding psychological and social factors that impact the brain's ability to learn. In this chapter, we focus on issues that are either new or changing due to brain adaptations. There is no better place to begin than by understanding how students gain and lose the motivation to learn.

## REWARD DEFICIENCY SYNDROME

It has long been known that much of human behavior is reward driven. How we sleep, eat, and even propagate is all dependent on the brain's reward system. A region in the brain known as the nucleus accumbens has been associated with reinforcing sleeping and eating habits and susceptibility to addictions. The nucleus accumbens came to the forefront in brain research because of its role in addiction. It was commonly thought that most people develop addictions by consistently overindulging in any substance that triggers a rush of dopamine in the nucleus accumbens. Over time, individuals would develop a tolerance that forced them to continually need to consume more to get the same level of reward they originally felt. Later, it was discovered that a small segment of the population was already at a greater risk of addiction because they suffer from a phenomenon known as *Reward Deficiency Syndrome* (Blum, 1989; Cloninger, 1983; Stice, Yokum, Bohon, Marti, & Smolen, 2010).

Individuals with Reward Deficiency Syndrome appear to have fewer dopamine D2 receptors in the nucleus accumbens. The result is lower dopamine activity in everyday life. There is a level of dopamine that individuals must maintain to exhibit self-control and be goal oriented. Dopamine deficiency is life altering. Students require appropriate levels of dopamine to be motivated to get up and go to school, to avoid being distracted by peers, and to value long-term goals over immediate gratification.

If individuals with dopamine deficiency consume a substance that triggers dopamine D2, they will instantaneously have a stronger drive to consume higher levels. Because they are born with a built-in tolerance, they immediately will have to consume more and more to obtain the original high. Later, this same deficiency was associated with emotional disorders. The theory is that the inability to get dopamine reinforcement from engaging in healthy practices produces the need to engage in high-risk behaviors to gain dopamine reinforcement. Some consistent features of emotional disorders are disturbed eating and sleeping patterns. It is now thought that these disturbances are due to the role of the nucleus accumbens. It is estimated that 20 percent of the world population suffers from Reward Deficiency Syndrome.

## THE ROLE OF DOPAMINE

Recent studies have made a correlation between the dopamine response and the drive to succeed and to learn (Schultz, 2007). Neuroscientist Kent Berridge, PhD, of the University of Michigan, states, "dopamine is needed to use already learned information to generate successful motivated performanc" (2006). For example, research conducted by Miller and associates at the Massachusetts Institute of Technology (MIT), determined that correct responses are rewarded with a release of dopamine. Immediately after receiving this reinforcement, the neurons in the prefrontal cortex and basal ganglia become stronger; thereby supplying more information because of improved electrical impulses (Puig & Miller, 2012). The prefrontal cortex and basal ganglia are involved in obtaining internal goals—in other words, the chemical signature for self-motivation. They are also vital players in learning and long-term memory. However, incorrect answers receive no chemical motivation to get questions correct in the future. This means that educators affect learning and memory every day by how they promote success or failure. The neurons involved in successfully answering a question retain the memory associated with the accomplishment, paving the way for continued success. In actuality, because of its correlation to dopamine, the correct answer creates a craving for additional correct answers.

The amygdala, the emotional brain, possesses three hardwired drives: to be safe, to be wanted, and to be successful. These three needs have been found to be present in every healthy human being. However, chemical imbalance in the brain can alter the presence of these drives. For example, individuals suffering from severe autism do not possess the drive to be wanted. Likewise, sociopaths do not have the drive to be safe or to be wanted. However, the drive to be successful seems to be present to some degree in even the most atypical brains. The challenge is that the need to be successful is intricately tied to emotions. We were created to strive to succeed. This drive remains intact as long as we experience more success than failure, but repeated failure begins to lower the dopamine response required to maintain motivation. The loss of motivation to succeed may trigger unhealthy emotional responses that can become habitual. Many students who exhibit habitual negative behaviors do so due to a lack of being successful at school.

The loss of motivation to learn is not simply about academic success. The human brain is designed to reward learning, not because of academic pursuits, but rather to survive. The brain rewards learning because it continues to expand one's cognitive reserve and protect the brain throughout one's life. The healthy longevity of the brain requires consistent learning at an advanced pace. Each time you learn the brain changes structurally and functionally for the better. A healthy dopamine response system is required not only for exceptional achievements, but also to engage in habits associated with success. The discipline required to study, practice a sport, advance a skill, and even go to work daily would not occur without dopamine reinforcement. A healthy brain is designed to maintain and fine-tune by consistently learning new things on a daily basis. Therefore, students who have lost the motivation to learn are more likely to fail not only in school, but also in life. Their health depends on the wonderful transformation that is induced by daily learning.

The research done by Davis and associates (2008) on athletes discovered that after experiencing a win, the region of the brain that plans future action (the premotor cortex) is motivated to practice those acts associated with achieving success. However, when the athlete experiences a failure, this same region appears inhibited. This is not to say that occasional losing or challenges are not a positive thing. It merely states that a pattern of failure produces the loss of future planning to improve. Occasional failure can be overcome, but only for those possessing a healthy brain. This is why cognitive neuroscientist Ian Robertson said, "Success and failure shape us more powerfully than genetics and drugs" (Robertson, 2012). Over time, success or failure changes our brain structure and chemical makeup, either making us smarter and better able to take on challenges or more ill-equipped to handle life's daily tasks.

## THE ROLE OF EDUCATION

How should educators respond to this research? The emphasis on grades produces a system in which there are perceived winners and losers. The response cannot be the lowering of standards and the fabrication of artificial success. Likewise, the answer is not the total revamping of the entire education system. However, educators cannot ignore these findings and maintain the status quo. Scientific research itself might have already provided a viable strategy toward how to promote success in learning. A study conducted by psychologist Clancy Blair (2002) determined that the greatest predictor of academic success was not intellect but the ability to self-regulate. Even more encouraging was that Blair discovered that students could change the trajectory of their lives by improving self-control.

Students can improve self-control by improving their abilities to focus. When the brain maintains focus on one thing, it is strengthening the areas of the brain that produce self-control. Therefore, improving focus is a concrete strategy for improving self-control. Students can improve attention through focus training and help put an end to the cycle of failure. There are many online sites that provide drills that have been shown to improve focus. Studies have shown that these drills can help improve focus as long as they are done for a few minutes each day. However, there are also many low-tech ways to improve focus. An individual merely has to study an object for sixty seconds without focusing on anything else, and then write down every detail he or she remembers about the object when not looking at it. Focusing on one object for a few minutes each day will help improve focus in just a few weeks. A person can read a book for 30 minutes daily without engaging in any form of multitasking. Singular focus on any task improves the brain's ability to focus. The dramatic new problem facing schools today is that even students who are not suffering from chemical imbalances need to improve their abilities to focus due to their constant interaction with technology, which diminishes this ability.

Advancements in technology and students' persistent daily interaction with electronic devices are having a negative impact on the brain's ability to focus, resulting in a diminished capacity to exhibit self-control. Surfing the web, watching videos, texting, e-mailing, working on laptops or tablets, taking photos, recording, or listening to music on their devices are examples of these interactions. Often students engage in many of these activities simultaneously. The ramifications of these behaviors are an increasing desire for stimulation that can result in an inability to focus on anything for an extended period of time. In addition, research shows that this loss of the ability to focus also increases emotional instability.

Gary Small, MD, Professor of Psychiatry at the David Geffen School of Medicine at UCLA, and colleagues conducted a neuroimaging study evaluating the brain's activity when individuals are engaged in surfing the web compared to reading a book. All the brain regions that are engaged when reading a book double in activation when surfing the web.

The natural assumption is that activities that cause this level of initial stimulation often experience a reduction in brain activity once the practice becomes more familiar. However, just the opposite occurred with individuals surfing the web. The activity of conducting online searches not only maintained high levels of stimulation, but stimulation levels heightened with increased exposure. The dilemma is that when the adapting brain quickly becomes conditioned to that level of stimulation, it continues to seek out more. Brains conditioned to this high level of stimulation will struggle to maintain focus when engaged in low-stimulation tasks such as reading a book, listening to a lecture, or writing a paper. Small's conclusion is that constant interaction with technology runs the risk of reducing the brain's ability to focus on one task and even creates a form of behavioral addiction (Small & Moody, 2009).

Some clever teachers reading this book might ask, why not put textbooks on tablets and merely conform to the changing brain? Such conformity will fail because the brain's desire for constant stimulation requires exposure to novel stimuli every few minutes. As a result, a book—even if placed on a tablet—will encounter a drop in focus in a matter of minutes. This explains why individuals who constantly surf the web average less than sixty seconds per site.

In 2009, Nass and two colleagues published findings concluding that people who engage in multitasking through the use of technological devices are unable to pay attention as well as individuals who limit their interaction with multiple forms of technology (Ophir, Nass, & Wagner, 2009). The study determined that the more individuals engage in multitasking using technology, the lower their ability to maintain focus. Individuals will mask this type of brain adaptation by merely participating in multiple things at one time so that their brains can continuously skip from task to task. This deludes them into thinking they are getting more done at one time. The reality is that the brain is incapable of multitasking. The brain cannot engage in several tasks simultaneously; it actually skips from one task to another at rapid rates of speed. However, during the switching between tasks, the performance of all tasks suffers. Nass's conclusion was, "multitaskers are lousy at multitasking."

After his initial study on multimedia multitaskers, Nass and colleagues began studying the effects of chronic technology multitasking—texting, searching the web, watching YouTube videos, and so on—on the developing brain. In 2012, he published findings that preteen girls who spend large amounts of time multitasking with digital devices tend to be less successful with social and emotional development. The drop in social behavior negatively impacted empathy as well as higher-level thinking (Pea et al., 2012).

Let's put these findings in practical terms. The brain is placid and changes in a unique way from persistent experiences in both structure and function (Hensch, 2004; Neville, Marquez, Taylor, & Pakulak, 2009). The student who is unable to do homework without listening to music finds himself constantly checking his cell phone, while having the laptop open to multiple sites. The student tells himself that the music and other devices help maintain focus because when not multitasking he quickly tires of the task. The truth is that the student can no longer focus on low-sensory homework assignments and has surrounded the activity with high-sensation components to get the sensory fix he so desperately needs. The result is homework performed at a standard below the student's abilities. This drop in performance is not noted by teacher, student, or parent because the higher standard achieved when focusing was never established.

Recent studies have shown that the ability to focus not only is crucial in carrying out cognitive tasks, but also insulates the brain from developing emotional problems. The reduction in the ability to focus has now been associated with an increased risk of depression, anxiety, panic disorders, and phobias. The loss of the ability to focus not only lowers self-control, but also lowers emotional control. Maintaining emotional control is essential to expressing all forms of self-control.

All is not lost. Schools have begun to conduct simple focus exercises with students that can help restore the brain's ability to maintain concentration and improve self-control. In schools that consistently perform focus drills with students, teachers report increased on-task behavior and improved academic performance. Similar focus exercises have been successfully utilized in studies that demonstrate both cognitive and emotional improvement through this type of brain training. For example, Amishi Jha, Associate Professor of Psychology at the University of Miami, and colleagues in 2010, had Marines who were performing in high-risk jobs participate in focus exercises for 12 minutes a day for 8 weeks. The Marines who engaged in the focus exercises were found not only to have improved memory capacity, but also to have better mood stability and performance under pressure compared to the control group.

A longitudinal study conducted over 20 years indicates that one of the long-term benefits of engaging in focus exercises is the improved connection between the brain's structures intricately involved with producing self-control. The connections associated with improved cognitive performance and insulation from emotional disorders become more intricately linked. The stronger the connections between the prefrontal cortex, parietal cortex, and insula, the better an individual's ability to maintain emotional stability, improve decision making, and maintain focus (Luders et al., 2012).

Many teachers are attempting to educate the current generation through lecturing, reading, and writing assignments. Many of the students who desire to attend to these tasks find themselves unable to because they are in need of greater levels of sensory stimulation.

Do not interpret the above-mentioned findings as a call to put technology back in the box. The desired outcome is to help teachers become aware of both the benefits as well as the unintended consequences related to technology. Knowledge is power; therefore, the information provided can be used to better equip teachers to help students thrive with the use of technology and not succumb to any of the ill effects. As with many advancements, there are precautions put in place once dangers are identified. For example, the advancement of being able to text on a cell phone placed drivers at risk when they attempted to text while driving. As a result, a national campaign was launched to educate drivers on the dangers of texting while driving, and some states implemented laws to prohibit the practice. Teachers can begin to promote a more successful future with technology by taking a few simple steps to educate students.

- Educate students on the impact that successful learning has on the human brain and how constant interaction with technology negatively impacts the brain's capacity. Consider including the following key points in the lesson:
  - How multitasking with technology can lower empathy
  - Why the increased use of technology can reduce the ability to delay gratification
  - The overarching impact of diminished focus can result in the inability to self-regulate, which is the greatest predictor of success.

- Train students to improve their brain's ability to focus by dedicating 60 seconds at the beginning of class to conduct simple focus exercises that will help their brains regain the ability to maintain concentration.
- Inform students of the need to spend an hour a day unplugged.
- Help students understand the importance of doing some single task activities to protect the brain.
  - For example, when doing homework, identify one subject that will be done without multitasking: no listening to music, surfing the web, texting, or e-mailing.

The goal is to shift the paradigm in education from focusing on failure to focusing on success. Teachers need to make students aware that the school's primary goal is to ensure that every student will be successful. This message must go beyond telling students that they can succeed to taking active measures to increase self-control. Students who improve their abilities to focus will experience greater self-control of emotions, behaviors, and the ability to remain on task. Experiencing academic success will increase dopamine, thereby producing a motivation for continued learning and increased life opportunities.

## HOW TO PROMOTE SELF-CONTROL AND FOCUS

Now that educators are aware of the significance that self-control plays in predicting student success, it is incumbent on teachers to help students develop self-control. In the same way that core information is the foundation of advanced learning, self-control is the foundation of a student's ability to be productive. It is almost unethical to observe so many students struggling to focus at a level required for learning and to continue to limit the range of responses to only academic interventions. Many studies have already shown that building capacity might be required before developing a skill for underperforming students. For example, Kraus and colleagues studied high school students from inner-city Chicago and matched them by reading ability, IQ, and the speed of auditory nerve activation. Half the students were placed in a junior reserve officers' training course. The other half was placed in a music-training program that focused on sight reading, playing technique, and music performance. In a follow-up assessment conducted 2 years later, students who received music training had faster speech-in-noise stimulus (the ability to decode discrete sounds better) (Kraus & Chandrasekaran, 2010).

A well-known problem of many inner-city children is that they do not hear or say words correctly. The lack of auditory accuracy means they will have problems recognizing words, spelling words, and associating words to their meaning. The inability to accurately distinguish sounds is a fundamental problem with the brain's capacity. There is no better example about the need to address capacity building than the research done by Patricia Kuhl (2011), who used advanced brain scanning devices to measure phonetic processing abilities of infants during their first year of life. Based on the consistency of her research outcomes, Patricia believes that studying phonetic processing in infants is easier than assessing them in adults. Infants are born with the ability to process every phonetic sound associated with every dialect. Once a baseline is established, the researchers can easily track the loss in the ability to efficiently process phonetic sounds not commonly heard in the infant's native language as well as the increased speed in processing of phonetic sounds common to the infant's native language.

The researchers found that the ability to accurately process sounds during the first year is predictive of the level of language skills displayed between 18 and 30 months of age. However, the more surprising finding was that phonetic skills during the first year were also predictive of language abilities and preliteracy skills at the age of 5. Perhaps the most extraordinary finding was that infants from poor socioeconomic backgrounds consistently performed lower on phonetic testing, which correlated to poor brain activation in areas related to language and literacy by age 5 (Kuhl, 2011). These findings further support the need to address the brain's capacity rather than merely limiting education's response to academic strategies. Students who do not process discrete language sounds will be negatively impacted in the areas of speech pronunciation, spelling, and reading for the rest of their academic careers. Music training helps address brain capacity concerns by correcting auditory issues and, as a result, improving academic performance in many areas, especially reading. Education's response to struggling students has been the definition of insanity—doing the same thing over and over again and expecting different results.

This section on self-control provides teachers with a strategy that improves the brain's capacity to control behavior rather than focusing only on managing or disciplining behaviors due to a lack of control. Historically there are three widely accepted methods for helping students improve their self-control. The first and most familiar is the insight-oriented approach to understanding the cause of the negative emotion and learning how to manage these feelings. The benefit of this approach has been studied and proven to be effective. Talking about the negative feelings slowly allows the brain to process these emotions in the region of the brain responsible for logic and reason rather than in the emotional center of the brain responsible for impulsive behaviors. Over time, the brain is conditioned to deal with certain emotional issues in a more thoughtful manner.

There are several drawbacks to this approach. The most significant drawback is that the process takes a long time. In some cases, it can take years, and individuals with the most severe emotional disorders seem most resistant to this process. Often those who suffer from impulsive behaviors are unable to understand why they engage in the behaviors and are even less capable of knowing what they can do to stop the behaviors. In addition, the ability to accurately process language is compromised by a chemical imbalance in the brain. This means that students struggling with severe emotional disorders are often the same individuals who have difficulty internalizing what has been said and altering behavior. These same profile students tend to manipulate the knowledge gained in therapy to avoid taking responsibility and receiving consequences for their actions.

The second method for improving self-control is learning coping strategies designed to lower heart and blood rate known as the *body calming method*. For example, students with anger issues or who suffer from anxiety are often taught deep breathing exercises. This strategy helps restore the body's equilibrium without focusing on the root cause of the problem. Functional Magnetic Resonance Imaging (fMRI) studies have shown that this method positively impacts the brain immediately and long term. The immediate impact is that lowering the heart rate has a calming effect on the amygdala. The long-term impact is the improvement of the brain's overall functioning by restoring greater control to the cortextual region, which is in charge of executive functioning. Studies show that the ability to slow one's breathing and meditate increases the high-frequency electroencephalography (EEG) electrical activity in gamma band, which improves the ability to focus (Lutz, Slagter, Dunne, & Davidson, 2008).

There are some drawbacks to this approach as well. The approach requires the ability to focus on one thing while blocking out distractions. When students are in an aroused state, they become hypersensitive to stimuli and struggle to block out things in their environment. Also, when in a state of arousal they are less able to stop thinking about what is troubling them to engage in these techniques effectively. Students suffering from Attention Deficit Hyperactivity Disorder (ADHD) struggle with this approach due to the nature of their disorder. Once students are trained in this method, they still have to overcome their disbelief that it can help them. Some students report that this technique makes them feel self-conscious and embarrassed.

The third way of promoting self-control is to help the brain shift immediately into a cognitive process. Since the human brain cannot focus on two things simultaneously, the individual learns to refocus the brain by doing very specific cognitive tasks to slow distractions and negative emotions. This approach shares many of the same benefits of the body calming method but is a concrete task that is easier to teach. Individuals who struggle to focus seem to be better able to engage in concrete tasks.

However, there are drawbacks to this approach as well. The strategies have to be regularly practiced. Students who struggle with self-control may initially need help in remembering to employ these strategies. Students have to be trained to complete the tasks at a high rate of speed for the appropriate amount of time to enable the brain to learn self-control. Students will have to be convinced that the process will help them, or they will not utilize it.

The supplement to this chapter includes a lesson for teachers on introducing and promoting self-control and focus in the classroom.

# CHAPTER 7 SUPPLEMENT PROMOTING SELF-CONTROL AND FOCUS

## GRADES 6–12

*(Teacher notes are in bold italics)*

This lesson is designed to help teachers introduce the concept of mental shift in a manner that increases student participation.

## THE LESSON GOALS

1. To provide a platform to enable students to understand and implement coping strategies as part of their daily lives when attempting to regain self-control.

2. To introduce specific coping strategies that have been proven through studies using fMRI to shift the brain into a more balanced state.

3. To provide approaches that will enable students to practice these strategies on a regular basis.

## MATERIALS

- Index cards
- Interesting objects
- Creative reinforcers
- Calming music selection

## THREE STRATEGIES TO PROMOTE MENTAL SHIFT

Each of the three strategies described in this section are often referred to as *sense grounding* techniques. Before beginning the lesson, it is important for teachers to become familiar with sense grounding and even practice the activities themselves.

## TECHNIQUE I—MENTAL GROUNDING

Mental grounding can be achieved by having a person rapidly list as many items as possible under a designated category within a given time frame. Getting individuals to recall items quickly within a given category in rapid succession forces the brain to shift from the emotional region to the executive functioning regions. It is important that the listing of items under a few different categories be done consecutively to allow the brain enough time to make the transition. This means that someone who is becoming agitated can have an active method to shift from focusing on the negative emotion to engaging in a concrete task. Since the technique is concrete rather than abstract, the individual is able to rate how well he or she attended to the action.

The following are a few examples of mental grounding:

- Identify as many colors as you can that are in the room.
- List as many square shapes as you can find in the room.
- Name as many cities as you can.
- Name as many TV shows as you can.
- Name as many music artists as you can.

Students can even create new categories in advance that they will use the next time they feel themselves becoming emotional. The key is that they have practiced the technique enough to be able to begin and have success in attending to the task during early stages of arousal.

## TECHNIQUE II—SOOTHING GROUNDING

Soothing grounding gets the individual to shift the condition of the emotional brain by focusing on topics that have a positive impact on them. It requires the individual to recall a series of positive things. The technique is most useful with individuals who have been trained to visualize. However, with individuals who are not trained to visualize, it works more like mental grounding. If a person can bring back what something looks like, smells like, or tastes like, this approach can quickly change his or her mood. The following are examples of soothing grounding.

I want you to close your eyes and think of the following things as I mention them:

- Your favorite thing to eat and how it tastes
- The last movie you watched that made you laugh

- Your favorite song. Now sing the first verse and chorus in your mind.
- A game you play that makes you happy

If students have not been trained to visualize, you can do similar things in list form.

List the following:

- Your favorite foods
- Your favorite TV shows
- The cars you would like to drive
- Your favorite songs

Please note that soothing grounding done in list form must be much longer than the example provided above.

Teachers should not attempt to have students engage in soothing grounding as a visualization exercise unless they have established a trusting classroom climate. Unless students feel safe and comfortable with their peers, they will struggle with feeling self-conscious and with closing their eyes. Sometimes dimming the lights and soft music in the background improves success. With more at-risk student populations, one might have to do soothing grounding one-on-one away from peers to get students comfortable with the process before doing it as a group. However, the listing approach to soothing grounding can be utilized with relative ease with most students.

## TECHNIQUE III—PHYSICAL GROUNDING

Physical grounding is really examining an object and identifying even the smallest details. Physically engaging in inspection is such a concrete task that the brain can quickly shift because you have to touch the object. It engages the senses and then shifts to a cognitive task. Although you can have students examine any object, it is more effective if the initial times you do this process, the students inspect something interesting or that they might be curious about. It is important that the teacher clearly illustrate the level of detail that students must achieve. See the detail provided below.

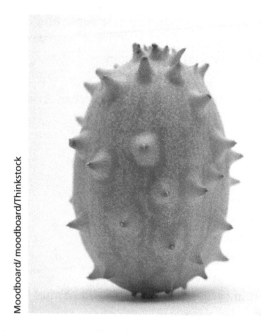

Moodboard/ moodboard/Thinkstock

Horned Melon:

- Bright orange, red, and yellow on top
- Green on the bottom
- Horns are pointy
- The tips of the horns are hard and white
- About the size of a baseball
- Feels prickly and firm
- The inside is the texture of Jell-O
- The inside is bright green
- The inside is filled with white seeds each encased in a green gel
- Texture in your mouth is like a crunchy Jell-O
- Tastes like a cucumber

## HOW TO INTRODUCE SENSE GROUNDING TO STUDENTS IN A CLASSROOM SETTING

Sense grounding is built on the fact that the brain cannot focus on two things simultaneously. If an activity can get the brain to focus on something else for a brief period of time, then when one reconsiders negative emotions, they have dissipated to some degree. The key here is to help students experience that this approach does, in fact, help them feel better.

At the beginning of class, have students rate their emotions on a scale of 1 to 10 using the following chart on an index card. Note: The words used to define emotions on this scale should be adapted for younger or lower-functioning students. On one side of the index card in the right-hand corner, they will put the letter "B" and their emotional numerical rating.

| 10 | Exploding |
|----|-----------|
| 9  | Boiling   |
| 8  | Angry     |
| 7  | Irritated |
| 6  | Stressed  |
| 5  | Nervous   |
| 4  | Indifferent |
| 3  | Tired     |
| 2  | Relaxed   |
| 1  | Happy     |

Once students have completed their emotional rating, have them set the cards aside. Then the teacher transitions into a sense grounding activity. Many times when introducing students to a new activity like sense grounding, it is better to present it in the form of a game. The rationale is that students who lack emotional control are reluctant even to attempt things that are designed to help them with their issues.

The teacher tells students the following rules to the activity:

- You can begin only when I say go.
- When I say stop, all pens and pencils must be placed on the desk and not touched again.
- The three students with the top cumulative scores at the end of the activity will win a prize. ***The teacher selects a reinforcer***.

Teacher note: The rationale for making the activity a contest is that it will be easier to motivate students as long as the correct motivator is used. This will help focus students on doing the activity. A teacher must assess if students are fully engaged in the activity because it will impact the outcome.

There will be a timer on the screen counting down from 60 to 0. After the clock counts down to 0, listen for the next assignment, and the clock will start again.

1. List as many TV shows as you can in 60 seconds—GO. *After 60 seconds, say, STOP.*

2. List as many musical artists as you can in 60 seconds—GO. *After 60 seconds say, STOP,*

3. List as many cities as you can in 60 seconds—GO. *After 60 seconds, say STOP.*

Add the total items you listed from your three lists and place it at the top of your paper. Have students switch papers and double-check the count. Then students review the list and identify any response that they think is inaccurate. The teacher has the final decision on whether an answer is correct. The teacher might want to have access to the Internet to verify certain answers. The teacher then validates the top three scores. Please note that the strategy of introducing the activity in a game format should be done only during the initial lesson. Students often struggle with participating in new activities, and introducing actions in a game format helps focus their brains on completing the task.

Once the scoring is completed, have students turn over their index cards and rate their emotional condition again using the same emotional rating scale. On the whiteboard, chart each student's emotional condition before and after the activity. Only the scores should be recorded; no identifying information should be on the cards or whiteboard. See example below:

| Before | After |
|--------|-------|
| 8 | 7 |
| 6 | 6 |
| 4 | 2 |
| 2 | 2 |
| 7 | 7 |

What usually occurs is that individuals' scoring 5 to 10 improve in their emotional rating. It is highly likely that little to no improvement will happen after you do the sense grounding activity only once. Merely maintain a record of the scores and end the activity. Once you have done the activity with students several times and note that their emotional scores are finally improving, it will be time to do the second half of the lesson.

Since this approach should be done at least once a week during morning meetings or homeroom activity, it will allow students opportunities to practice the technique regularly so that it can ultimately be utilized when stressed.

## PART II—PROBLEM SOLVING

You will notice that a lot of you were not as angry, upset, or irritated after doing this activity as you were before. ***Show students the pattern in the scores from past activities.*** Let's help you understand why.

1. The human brain can focus only on one thing at a time. You might think you are focusing on more than one thing at the same time, but what your brain is really doing is switching from one thing to another and then back so fast that you cannot notice. So if you can get your brain to focus on something else, you can trick the brain into feeling a little better.

2. When you think about what bothers or upsets you, it triggers a specific part of the brain that deals with emotions. When you think about things that are not emotional, it occurs in the part of the brain that makes thoughtful decisions. The part of your brain that deals with emotion does not think before doing things, so that part of the brain makes poor decisions. Thus, when we get the emotional brain offline and get the part of the brain that makes better decisions online, we gain self-control and make better decisions.

3. Activities like the one we did this morning improve the brain's ability to increase focus. Research has indicated that one negative effect of always engaging with technology is the diminishing loss of the ability to focus. Thus, your brain needs to practice on focusing on one thing for some concentrated minutes to remain healthy.

So why did I have you do this activity? Because doing detailed lists quickly in succession tricks the brain to turn off the emotional brain and turn on the rational brain. That means when you are getting upset, this is something you can do to help control your emotions. Think of a topic and make a quick list. Then think of another and make a quick list. Just keep on doing it for a while and regain control. Anything that improves self-control or focus is good for the brain.

This is a good skill to practice, so at the beginning of class, we will do different exercises that help the brain switch from the emotional brain to the rational brain, which will also improve focus. We will learn these techniques and practice them. The reason we need to practice them regularly is because the better you do this, the easier it will be to do when you are upset and it will improve your focus.

## WHY IS IT IMPORTANT TO HAVE WAYS TO MANAGE OUR EMOTIONS?

Characteristics of the emotional brain (the amygdala):

- Impulsive
- Does not think
- Cuts you off from your thinking
- Takes control until you are calm, by that time it is often too late
- Repeats bad decisions of the past

Everyone has times when they get so upset they lose control. Usually, the outcomes from those experiences are negative. The most successful people have a set of things they do when they begin to get upset that helps them calm down, so their thinking brain stays on. The goal for every student in this school is to learn ways to keep our thinking brains on so we can have success. Think about some of the things that happen to students when they let their emotional brain take control:

- Arguing
- Yelling
- Fighting
- Suspensions
- Expulsion
- Arrest
- Legal problems
- Lost relationships
- Substance use
- Alternative education placement
- Alternative home placement

Imagine if you knew a way to maintain control, how different your life could be. We are trying to teach you how to manage yourself so others do not think they have to help manage you.

Then do the following steps:

1. Name the technique: So what is a good name to call this technique? Brainstorm possible names and then select one. *The reason you have students name the technique is that they will be less likely to think it is corny if it is called something they like. It is also a good idea to prompt students that you will attempt to remind them to use this approach when you notice that they are getting upset in the future.*

2. Select a gesture: Identify a gesture that can be used to remind us to practice the technique in the classroom when needed. Brainstorm possible gestures and then select a gesture. *A gesture is great because you do not have to say anything to trigger the behavior. The brain responds to gestures better than to language when upset.*

3. Choose a visual cue: Identify a visual cue that can be posted in the classroom to help remind us of what we have learned and to implement this technique when needed. Brainstorm possible visual cues and then select one. Make a poster (maybe in art class to post in the room). *The visual cue in the classroom has been found to help students remind themselves to utilize this strategy.*

Do the mental grounding technique with students several times until they demonstrate they can do it proficiently. Remember, you cannot ask students to do a new behavior when they are upset, unless they have done it consistently when they are calm. Once students have mastered the mental grounding technique, then introduce another sense grounding method. It is important to constantly repeat the fact that students have the power to control their emotions by using these techniques. It is also a good idea to occasionally reward students when they use the techniques and are able to avoid engaging in negative behaviors. Once all the techniques have been learned, then practice them interchangeably throughout the school year to achieve mastery.

# The Paradox of the Slow and Gifted Learner

Monkeybusinessimages/iStock/Thinkstock

**THIS CHAPTER**

How we perceive and treat students plays a significant role in how they behave and perform. This chapter illustrates just how similar the brains and behaviors are between two student profiles considered to be polar opposites. The sad reality is that many of the most brilliant minds go undiscovered because they were shaped by adult misperceptions and beliefs.

## INITIAL PERCEPTION OF SELF COMES FROM OTHERS

The topic of academic success cannot be addressed without examining how the perception of being smart is developed and how it impacts the human brain and behavior. In the early years of life, a child's perception of self comes from others, mainly from parents or caregivers but also from other adults who are consistently involved in the child's life. It should not be surprising that adults play a significant role in how smart a child thinks he or she is. Many adults are aware of their conscious behaviors that help shape this perception; however, grownups are often unaware of the subconscious and unconscious behaviors that drive a sense of self. From the most successful to the least successful student, the perception of self begins to set a trajectory for life outcomes.

The paradox is that labeling children as a slow or gifted learner places too much emphasis on being smart. Struggling students believe they are not smart enough to take on challenging subject matter and tend to give up easily. They believe that they can never master the challenge and, therefore, avoid putting forth the effort required. Gifted children who have glided effortlessly through the lower grades often do not encounter their first academic challenge until middle school. By that time, they have come to believe that being smart means never having to struggle. Not having experienced academic challenge early enough creates a false expectation of what being smart is. This false expectation can produce a sudden bout of anxiety when the work is not easily mastered and internal fear that they might not be as smart as they have been told. As a result, the gifted learners might not seek help but rather feign a lack of interest in school or engage in negative behaviors to avoid letting anyone know that they are struggling.

## THE INHERENT DRIVE TO SUCCEED

The natural drive that motivates the response of both the struggling and the gifted student is the need to feel successful. As mentioned earlier, the amygdala, the part of the brain in charge of emotions, has three universal needs: the need to feel safe, the need to feel wanted, and the need to be successful. The need to succeed is so powerful that when it is not met, it can produce intense emotional behavior. Children who are told by their parents that they cannot succeed would rather play the part of the unmotivated student or demonstrate behavioral problems than cope with having tried and failed. Children told by parents and teachers alike that they are smart will often create excuses for the sudden drop in academic performance rather than tell anyone that they cannot understand the work. The surprising outcome is that both struggling students and gifted learners often choose to play the part of the unmotivated or belligerent student rather than let the world know the emotional reasons for their behaviors—fear of failure.

Extended periods of failure for both the struggling and the gifted learner can produce such chemical instability that the result is real behavioral and emotional problems. If the gifted learner's potential goes unidentified for too long, this student will become indistinguishable from the struggling student. Since the initial struggle often first begins for the gifted learner during middle school, it is easy for teachers who do not know the student well to miss how bright the child truly is. This is especially true for minority males who belong to underperforming subgroups. The existing bias that students from underperforming subgroups consistently struggle with academics makes it difficult for most teachers to see the potential of these gifted learners.

The solution for both the struggling student and the gifted child is exactly the same: creating ritualized nurturing environments in which students are more able to take risks. Predictable rituals improve the brain's chemical balance. It is the more chemically fragile struggling and gifted student who will be unable to cope with challenge appropriately. School environments that are highly structured can improve chemical functioning, thereby reducing emotional responses.

Nurturing environments, in this case, means places where it is safe to make mistakes. Although mistakes do not help the brain as much as success, schools need to diminish the stress associated with failure. From the first day at school, it is important for teachers to drive home to all students that school is a safe place to make mistakes. If it had not been for the ability to learn from mistakes and the willingness to keep on trying, we would have never flown across the skies or walked on the moon. The greatest mathematical, scientific, and engineering discoveries are all outcomes of our ability to learn from mistakes and never to have the mistakes stop us from trying again. However, this makeup is developed from consistent opportunities to succeed.

Modify the standard curriculum for a range of students—the accelerated to the slow learner. The technique is exactly the same, preparing the same subject matter for an upper-grade level and a younger-grade level. However, the key is not to set preconceived limitations on how far each student might be able to go in an area of interest. Once students experience success, it is important to allow them to build on it. The drive to succeed is so powerful that once struggling students find areas of interest, they will surprise you with how far they can go.

## TEACH STUDENTS ABOUT THE BRAIN

Teach students the truth about the brain. Help them understand the brain is like a muscle that can become smarter. Each student can build a stronger brain by learning. The harder they work, the faster it can grow. Many students believe that intelligence is a stagnant quotient, often because parents and teachers unknowingly establish that perception. For example, parents might remark that one child is not as smart as his brother. Well-intentioned teachers tell students that they are not all going to be good at math, or social studies, or English. Students interpret that message to mean that when you struggle with something it means that you will never be good at it. For some students who struggle in all academic areas, the message means that that they will not be good at school. However, the message should be that every student can get better at any subject if he or she works hard enough.

Teachers should remember that research determined that highly gifted individuals often display surprising weaknesses in specific academic areas. This means that many struggling students should not be quickly dismissed from being considered as gifted or extremely bright because they display significant academic shortcomings. One study discovered that gifted students can have specific learning deficits, struggle with focus and attention, and may be sensitive to logical contradictions in spelling causing them to perform poorly with the phonemics of spelling (Kuhl, Coffey-Corina, Padden, & Dawson 2005; Whitmore & Maker, 1985). In addition, the motor skills of many gifted students develop relatively slow, producing poor penmanship. Teachers who are unwilling to struggle through the inattentiveness, poor penmanship, and misspelled words might miss the next brilliant mind of our generation. It is not irrational to think that most struggling students might have at least one area of academic excellence because of how the human brain compensates for deficits. The reality is that many struggling and gifted students first appear as uncut gems that require success to bring out their brilliance. Students' potentials might be more frequently discovered if teachers viewed all pupils as gifted and provided them with every opportunity to prove that they are.

## RECOMMENDATIONS

1. Attempt to make sure all students will be successful on the first quiz or test given. This can be easily achieved by allowing students to demonstrate knowledge of test information in a range of ways. If a teacher has been associating symbols to key information, have them circle the correct symbol to the question without grading responses. Have students stand and demonstrate the correct gesture associated with the answer. Utilize some form of wireless poll response, which allows students to text on their phones the correct answer and immediately tallies the percentage of students who got each answer correct. This strategy allows students to gain feedback in a nonjudgmental manner.

2. Teach students about the brain so that they develop a basic understanding of how they learn best and that brain plasticity means that they can train their brains to be smarter. Brain plasticity means the brain can always change, based on what you train it to do.

3. Teachers who are aware of how the brain compensates for deficit areas should be on the lookout for skills or abilities every student possesses. A student who cannot spell and write legibly can be producing many advanced connections reflective of higher-ordered thinking. Without allowing that student to demonstrate knowledge in unconventional ways, this child could focus on his or her inadequacies and conclude that he or she is not good at schoolwork.

# 9

# Science of Cheating

## THIS CHAPTER

The current education climate of standardized testing might have created a subconscious and, at times, conscious motivation to cheat to succeed.

If adults are subconsciously less motivated to catch cheaters, then it is only logical to think that students will begin to perceive cheating as an approved behavior. The risk is a future generation willing to cut corners to achieve goals.

## HAS CHEATING LOST ITS STATUS AS AN INFRACTION?

Once you introduce a paradigm of success and students begin to like the feeling of winning, this can result in a magnified pressure to cheat. In a recent *train the trainer* program for teachers, I could not help but notice a high number of teachers cheating on the final exam. I clarified that this was not a group process and that it was to be perceived as a standard test. To my surprise, none of the teachers changed their behavior. In fact, they made no attempt to conceal their cheating or even to vary their answers. It occurred to me that the cheating behavior seemed to be becoming more prevalent over the course of the past few years.

During a recent school tour, I witnessed numerous students cheating on a test. The teacher was present. So I inquired if it was permissible to work with partners on this exam. The teacher sternly said that the students knew that cheating was a violation, and if caught, they would get a zero and their parents would be notified. Later, when conducting student interviews, I asked students if the cheating I witnessed was common. Surprisingly, a majority of students said yes, in certain classes where the teachers do not care.

I began to ponder if cheating had lost its status as a major infraction and if, for some reason, it was not only on the rise, but also becoming more accepted. The research on cheating is limited, but the findings that exist are considered to be widely accepted.

The first finding is that cheating is considered to be on the rise. A survey back in 1997 already indicated that students did not perceive cheating as a breach of ethical or moral code. This survey of 1,800 students conducted across nine state universities found that three-fourths of students admitted to cheating on tests and written assignments (McCabe & Treviño, 1997). A list of studies to determine that cheating within the general population is on the rise is not necessary. Even in fields where the integrity of findings can often result in life or death, the pressure to cheat seems to have increased. One-third of scientists engaged in research that had medical implications confessed to engaging in questionable research practices to secure or maintain funding (Martinson, Anderson, & de Vries, 2005).

At its root, cheating is about self-control. Self-regulation is the one mental process that overrides obstacles that hinder planning, attention, learning, memory, and coping required for students to achieve immediate goals and obtain long-term success. Without the skill to self-regulate, students will succumb to the whim of every thought, distraction, emotion, and desire. The lack of self-regulation is at the root of most of the behavioral and academic issues that schools face. Therefore, an increase in cheating should be viewed as a symptom of diminishing self-control. The development of self-control enables students to transcend immediate desires to delay gratification and replace them with thoughts and actions that promote academic success (Inzlicht, Bartholow, & Hirsh, 2015).

The ability to exercise self-regulation is dependent on the development of the prefrontal cortex to the point that it can exert control over the limbic system (primitive brain) (Bunge & Zelazo, 2006; Godefroy, Lhullier, & Rousseaux, 1996; Munakata et al., 2011; Robinson, Heaton, Lehman, & Stilson, 1980). A key reason schools should consider promoting self-control is because it has been found to be the greatest predictor of educational success (Blair, 2002). Self-regulation is developed during childhood but can also be advanced through late adolescence and even into early adulthood; however, there are fewer obstacles when developed early in life (Bédard, Lévesque, Bernier, & Parent, 2002; Carver, Livesey, & Charles, 2001; Leon-Carrion, García-Orza, & Pérez-Santamaría, 2004; Williams, Ponesse, Schachar, Logan, & Tannock, 1999). Helping students develop self-control during the primary grades changes the trajectory of their entire academic experience. The prefrontal cortex is developed in predictable environments, through positive social interactions and learning. Cheating is a shortcut produced by the inability of the prefrontal cortex to self-regulate.

## A CLIMATE FOR CHEATING

The reality is that we tend to think that most people do not cheat. However, research states that humans are actually quick to cheat if circumstances are conducive. In 2008, Dan Ariely of Duke University and his colleagues conducted a test with a group of college students in which they had already determined a baseline of academic math performance. They asked students to solve a math puzzle for a cash reward and constructed the assignment in a manner that cheating could not be detected. The researchers determined that the scores were not inflated by a few students cheating a lot but by many students cheating a little. The findings showed what we already know about humans; when circumstances are conducive, more individuals are apt to cheat (Gino, Ayal, & Ariely, 2009).

In one study, researchers found that when circumstances are not conducive, cheating is mostly done by creative males. (Gino & Ariely, 2012). This finding should not be surprising to every woman on the face of the Earth (men cheat). Individuals who score higher on psychological tests of creativity are more apt to be dishonest (Gino & Ariely, 2012). This is because they are better at self-deception, naturally come up with more ingenious ways to cheat, and, therefore, are under greater temptation to succumb to one of their ideas. In addition, men are overrepresented in crimes committed that involve cheating (Fang, Bennett, & Casadevall, 2013). Testosterone may also play a role in this disproportionate representation.

However, for those who are not creative males driven to cheat, the fear of loss has been identified as the strongest motivation to cheat—the fear of losing respect, status, love, employment, and so on. Studies done by neuroscientist R. Grant Steen (2011) indicate that incidents of cheating rise tenfold when the risk of losing something one values or requires is at stake.

Perhaps the biggest everyday influence to cheat is simply being in an environment where cheating is occurring because after a person participates in cheating once, it becomes easier the next time. Researchers had students take a vocabulary test without using a dictionary or thesaurus. Students were placed on their honor not to use either of the above-mentioned resources, while researchers observed through a one-way mirror. Students did not know that in each experiment group, someone was planted to model cheating. Once students observed that one individual cheating, they were three times more likely to cheat (Blachnio & Weremko, 2011). After repeating the study numerous times across various settings, the researchers concluded that cheating is infectious. This brings us to the Harvard scandal, in which 125 out of 279 students taking an Introduction to Congress class were investigated for cheating. More than half of those investigated were found guilty. It is highly unlikely that these students lack the acumen to do the work or that they were all creative males with a propensity to cheat. More likely, it is that the bending of the rule became so widespread and so well known by students that it became infectious. The only other possibility is that when one studies the behavior of members of Congress, one can become influenced to cheat.

Let's consider the climate established by standardized testing. It seems to meet all the criteria for creating an environment conducive for cheating. The adults who are supposed to instill ethics and be vigilant against the act of cheating might not be as motivated as they once were. There is a fear of loss present; teachers in schools that don't meet Adequate Yearly Progress risk loss of reputation, respect, and in some cases even employment. The emphasis on test performance placed on students no longer comes solely from parents and internal drive. With added pressure, students too are experiencing fear of loss, because more and more schools celebrate improved test scores through some form of extrinsic rewards. Students are told that who they are perceived to be is found in a test score.

When the pressures mount, a school climate might succumb to increased incidents of cheating. Once cheating increases, more students are apt to participate, and the behavior can escalate quickly. This might explain why I witnessed more teachers cheating when given a final exam. If they are in an environment that condones it, they are more apt to participate in the behavior themselves. It also might explain why students in some settings perceive that they are encouraged to cheat. It is not that humans are intrinsically bad, but that they will behave in a predictable manner under certain conditions.

## CONSEQUENCES OF CHEATING

For every behavior, there are consequences. If one of the unexpected consequences of an ill-conceived notion of mandatory testing is a generation willing to cut corners, we will all have lost. One of the jobs of teachers is to model and teach ethics, to help young minds see that at times the end does not justify the means. There is no better place for a student to learn that every achievement is altered by shortcuts. The one thing we can never regain is time. Every moment we miss learning something in the present alters what we could have learned in our lifetimes. It is important to remember that the human brain is transformed and improved through the process of learning. Every time students cheat themselves from having to learn something new, they alter the possibilities of what their minds could have achieved. In the case of learning, the end does not justify the means—the end is determined by the means.

## RECOMMENDATIONS

1. Teachers can diminish the desire to cheat by strengthening the prefrontal cortex through improved focus, memory, and learning.

   - Engage in focus drills.
   - Provide students with strategies to improve memory.

- For example, help students become aware of how the brain consolidates memories through repetition and quiet thought (an added benefit of being unplugged for at least 1 hour a day). Short-term memories are also more likely to become long-term memories when students employ proven strategies found to increase retention (see a few examples below).

  - Question and analyze the information immediately after learning.
  - Discuss the information with someone else using their own words.
  - Think of images that help visualize what they have just learned.
  - Explore and elaborate on the new information creating unique associations.

- Stress the fact that learning improves self-control.

2. Teachers should be aware that a focus on advancing test scores can subconsciously bias the brain to miss evidence of cheating. When we are aware of how the brain biases our subconscious minds, we can correct misperceptions.

3. Be aware that many students do not perceive cheating as morally wrong. At the beginning of each school year, it is important to explain to students why cheating harms them. If they are allowed to cheat, then more students will participate and think of cheating as no big deal. The habit of cheating is hard to break; therefore, in life's crucial moments cheaters tend to take shortcuts that can cost them dearly. An example of a pattern found in people who think cheating is not wrong is a chemist who has cut corners his or her entire academic career, changes the findings on a drug trial, and hundreds of people die.

4. Explain to students that individuals who take the time to learn things improve their brain's capacity in the future, even if the information is something they are not likely to use in the future.

# 10

# The Decline of Empathy

Ingram Publishing/Thinkstock

## THIS CHAPTER

The drop in empathy scores due to increased interaction with technology is having severe ramifications not only on social behavior, but also on academic achievement. It is crucial for educators to be aware of the issues and begin to address them before it becomes a pervasive problem.

## PLUMMETING EMPATHY SCORES

Educators are keenly aware of the fact that one of the roles of education is to teach positive social behavior. Schools offer social settings in which students are exposed to other students from different races, cultures, and backgrounds. The social aspect of academics is always present. Teachers face the impact of the social dynamics in every class during every lesson. Yet teachers are not often aware of the changes on a neurobiological level that are having a revolutionary impact on student social behavior.

Since empathy scores continue to plummet, Cohen's (2008) finding that social behavior and the desire for social approval play a significant role in producing higher-level thinking takes on greater importance. The movie *Mean Girls* depicted a group of well-adjusted affluent teens who behaved cruelly toward everyone who was not in their clique. The girls displayed the type of behaviors more commonly associated with maladjusted adolescents than honor roll students. However, cruel acts being committed by seemingly healthy children and adolescents seem to be on the rise. Is this trend real or just another example of how every older generation overestimates the negative behaviors of youth culture?

In this case, moms and dads might not be *crying wolf* and the *sky might actually be falling*—falling, just like the empathy levels have been among children and adolescents. Over the last three decades, self-reported empathy surveys reveal a significant decline in the trait among college-age students (Konrath, O'Brien, & Hsing, 2010). It is important to note that these surveys are conducted with college students who disproportionally represent a better-adjusted segment of our society's young adults. An alarming fact is that the downward trend in empathy scores has demonstrated a sharper decline in the last 10 years. This means that the issue is not stabilizing but rapidly increasing in severity. To make matters worse, surveys among the same population reveal that self-reported narcissism has reached new highs (Thomaes, Bushman, Orobio de Castro, & Stegge, 2009; Twenge 2006). Low empathy and high narcissism are frequent components of some of the more severe emotional disorders.

## WHY ARE EMPATHY SCORES FALLING?

What has caused the empathy index that had been so consistent until the seventies to trend downward suddenly and then dramatically drop?

A primary cause for this dramatic drop might be the role texting has played as a main means of communication among young people. Texting has replaced the phone as the communication method of choice for children, adolescents, and young adults.

*Empathy* is defined as the observation of an action, perception, or emotional state in an individual that activates a corresponding representation in the observer. A significant study on empathy concluded that empathic individuals exhibit subconscious mimicry of the postures, mannerisms, and facial expressions of others to a greater extent than nonempathic individuals (Porter et al., 2000). Later, a definitive study of empathy used functional magnetic resonance imaging (fMRI) to discover that when observing emotions in others, the motor areas of the brain simulate doing the same emotional cues in the brain (Carr, Iacoboni, Dubeau, Mazziotta, & Lenzi, 2003). This discovery suggests that internal imitation of someone else's action occurs in the brain and is an essential component of experiencing empathy.

Researchers also determined that individuals who externally mimic emotional cues experience heightened chemical signals that increase the understanding of another's emotional condition, thereby producing a higher level of empathy. Developmental research has demonstrated that motor and affective mimicry are active in the earliest interactions between infants and caregivers, indicating that processes might be hardwired. Although the capacity for empathy may be hardwired, an fMRI experiment confirmed that individuals are required to observe facial expressions, postures, hand movements, and tone of voice to trigger the activity in the brain regions that are implicated in empathy. The brain's ability to appropriately trigger empathy seems to require consistent exposure to the emotional nonverbal cues and tonality of others.

This same study determined that the brain regions included in empathy are

- the superior temporal sulcus, which plays a role in the imitation of other's behaviors;
- the anterior insula, which plays a role in interpreting and predicting the behaviors of others;
- the amygdala, which provides emotional meaning to nonverbal cues; and
- the premotor cortex, which plays a role in mirroring behaviors in the brain and social learning related to practices (Carr, McLaughlin, Giacobbe-Greico, & Smith, 2003).

Another contributing factor to lowering empathy scores could be related to the increased number of children and adolescents being exposed to violent media and video games. A common practice among teens is to videotape any act of cruelty and post it on the Internet as a form of entertainment. A study conducted by Bushman and Anderson (2009) demonstrated that empathy is temporarily lowered after exposure to violent media content. In the world of instant access, violent media is at every teen's fingertips. Due to this overexposure, we might be developing a certain level of callousness to gruesome acts. No longer do we mourn as a nation at mass shootings and senseless acts of violence since we see it almost every day. The human brain is placid and changes in both structure and function by our experiences; it has been proven that persistent exposure to violent stimuli will produce long-term structural change.

In 2006, Bruce Bartholow, a psychologist at the University of Missouri, and colleagues reported that chronic violent game players show less activation of a particular brain wave in response to violent images than nonviolent players do, indicating lower feelings of aversion. Psychologists are not claiming that exposure to video games produces sociopaths; however, there is a real risk to the dampening of empathy. Funk and her colleagues (2004) determined that the most consistent outcome from exposure to video games that portray real-life violence seems to be the dampening of the brain's ability to produce empathy. Remember, empathy also plays a significant role in our daily learning. Empathy is a form of embodied cognition.

## THE IMPACT OF LOWER EMPATHY ON COMPREHENSION

Therefore, this shift in empathy should be a concern for every educator. As empathy drops, so will the ability of students to glean more from literature than a grouping of words. The ability to comprehend at a gut level is actually the highest form of understanding. In addition, students who are callous to the feelings of others tend to undermine the school climate, which also negatively impacts learning and social development.

Humans have the capacity to adopt the subjective perspective of others intentionally by putting themselves in other people's shoes. This capacity requires the reader to be able to mentally simulate another's perspective using one's own neural machinery. A neuroimaging study had participants write a short story depicting real-life emotional situations that cause feelings such as shame (Ruby & Decety, 2004). While writing the story, participants were asked to imagine how someone they cared about would feel. The results indicated that writing, even from the perspective of another, triggers a cognitive process seen with empathy. However, the highest emotional processing of empathy, which includes the amygdala and the temporal poles was demonstrated when the writer had an existing emotional sensitivity to the scenario being written about.

This begins to explain why we are capable of seeing beauty in the written word or can be moved to tears by a poem. Therefore, empathy plays a significant role in daily learning. We have the unique ability to read or write a passage and feel the joy or pain that the words are attempting to convey. Niedenthal's work demonstrated that words standing alone tended not to evoke the same level of response in facial expressions in the brain as words read within a context (Niedenthal et al., 2009). Empathy's role is in comprehension. It is interesting to note that individuals who showed less facial flexing while reading also demonstrated lower levels of reading comprehension. These same individuals scored lower on empathy scales.

It is widely known that sociopaths and psychopaths lack empathy. They lack the ability to see someone else's pain and experience just a little of what the other individual is going through. The intelligent sociopath can become adept at reading nonverbal cues and can cognitively know what these expressions mean. However, comprehension is limited to merely cortextual understanding. When limited empathy is coupled with high narcissism, it produces manipulation of others and callousness toward the pain our actions cause others. It is this lack of being able to experience strong feelings in daily life that drive sociopaths to such extreme behaviors just to experience feeling something. Dr. Sean Mackey of the Stanford Systems Neuroscience and Pain Lab, said, "If it had not been for man's ability to experience empathy, man would have wiped each other off the face of the earth long ago" (Mirsky, 2008).

## RECOMMENDATIONS

Schools are not merely social settings—they are social training grounds. Within large social settings, the brain establishes normative behaviors through the repeated practices of the majority. The social practices within the walls of every school establish a social template for the future. The strongest influence on human behavior is social attraction. The amygdala is attracted to those it shares things in common with. Therefore, students' social behavior strongly influences their peers. However, social trends and patterns of current student behavior indicate a lowering of empathy and an increase in narcissism. Schools must help students learn that social behaviors are the most powerful predictors of physical health outcomes, the acquisition or prevention of risk factors, and the ability to accurately assess and empathize with human behavior (Adler et al., 1994; Berkman, 1995; Kiecolt-Glaser, McGuire, Robles, & Glaser, 2002; Uchino, 2004). Most important, developing healthy social practices will help students guard against the lowering of empathy due to constant interaction with technology, which is expediting acts of cruelty. The current trend in social behavior threatens the brain's capacity to feel the pain of others and to comprehend the depths that the spoken or written word can have.

## THE SOCIAL IMPORTANCE OF LUNCH

The research on the positive benefits of mealtime rituals is astounding. Schools should be very cognizant that there is a significant mealtime gathering that takes place in every cafeteria across America. It is crucial that schools promote an atmosphere in the lunchroom that allows the benefits of the social ritual of meals to be realized. A *social meal* is defined as appropriate conversation while dining. Study after study identifies the benefits of the social meal for children. The list of benefits include lowering the risk of obesity, smoking cigarettes, alcohol abuse, marijuana use, experimenting with illicit drugs or prescription drugs, and stress (The National Center on Addiction and Substance Abuse at Columbia University, 2011). In addition, the social meal has some vital social benefits, such as increasing communications between peers and with adults. Face-to-face conversations while eating triggers oxytocin, which is a hormone associated with bonding, lowering of stress, and improving cortextual functioning. Oxytocin's role in bonding coupled with empathy's role in meaningful conversation makes for a powerful daily experience that hones students' empathy skills.

## EDUCATE STUDENTS CONCERNING THE IMPORTANCE OF FACE-TO-FACE CONVERSATIONS

The increased role of texting in communication can reduce levels of empathy. Individuals are not born with empathy skills fully developed. The amygdala and the insula play a significant role in reading nonverbal cues and interpreting their meaning. Not that long ago researchers informed the world that babies are born with the capacity to replicate the linguistic sounds found in any dialect. This finding caused researchers to expose a cohort of children to tapes of various languages throughout their infancy to see if this would increase language capacity in adulthood. It had zero impact. We now know that an infant's focus on language dramatically increases when accompanied by a face. It is also known that empathy is triggered by the brain during face-to-face interactions. I am not recommending that students should not text, but that they understand the need to balance the behavior with sufficient face-to-face communication.

## INFORM PARENTS OF THE NEED TO PUT SOME LIMITATIONS ON ACCESS TO VIOLENT MEDIA CONTENT AND GAMING

No, they do not have to shield their child from the *real world*. However, they might want to put some restrictions regarding their child's amount of real-world exposure as it relates to violent media and violent video games. The research is clear; the negative effect on the human brain from violent content comes from persistent exposure.

The lowering of empathy will negatively impact social interactions and reading comprehension. In a world of diminishing empathy, I fear that fewer and fewer students will fully comprehend works like Shakespeare and Cummings. Yes, they may be able to read the words, but meaning in context requires the active process of empathy.

here is the deepest secret nobody knows

(here is the root of the root and the bud of the bud

and the sky of the sky of a tree called life; which grows

higher than the soul can hope or mind can hide)

and this is the wonder that's keeping the stars apart

(Cummings, 1994, © Trustees for the E.E. Cummings Trust)

# 11

# New Breed of Bully

Highwaystarz-Photography/iStock/Thinkstock

## THIS CHAPTER

Educators have begun to sense that bullying behaviors are changing. Thus, the definition of bullying has expanded to begin to tackle the evolution of cyberbullying. However, what seems to be missing in definition and response is a sound understanding about why bullying is changing. In the case of bullying, a better understanding will help shape a more effective response.

## THE INCREASE IN BULLYING BEHAVIOR AMONG GIRLS

The drop in empathy scores might best explain the new breed of bully that is taking place in schools. The scientific explanation of the famous nursery rhyme, *boys are made of frogs and snails and puppy-dog tails* is due to testosterone and a larger amygdala. Testosterone is the hormone that makes boys more physical, aggressive, and angry. The larger amygdala is responsible for increased competitiveness, aggression, and impulsive behaviors. This is why boys are more prone to lash out physically and engage in more physical forms of bullying. However, *girls are made of sugar and spice and everything nice* is explained by estrogen and a smaller amygdala. Estrogen is a peace-loving drug that increases communication and empathy. This along with a smaller amygdala seems to prevent girls from reaching a level of emotional loss of control that cuts off communication with the cortex as often happens with their male counterparts. As a result, a majority of girls are able to remain thinking even while emotional. Therefore, bullying practices commonly employed by girls often are more thoughtful and calculating.

Although the physical form of bullying is on the rise among girls, it still makes up a significantly lower ratio of female bullying practices. The increase in physical acts of bullying by girls can be partially attributed to increased levels of testosterone. Congenital Adrenal Hyperplasia (CAH) causes female fetuses to produce larger amounts of testosterone (Berenbaum & Bailey, 2003). Girls who produce higher levels of testosterone are often the tomboys who usually grow out of more masculine behaviors after puberty. However, many researchers think that CAH in conjunction with increased levels of testosterone in food, generations of women in the workforce competing with males, and access to more physical sports have all attributed to a small portion of girls having high enough testosterone levels to behave like *frogs, snails, and puppy-dog tails*.

Far more common and maybe even more sinister is the female bully who is calculating and cunning. Not driven by the need to be physically impulsive, for girls bullying takes on a common practice called *ostracizing*. School climate assessment data are quite definitive. High school cliques commonly target specific individuals with whom the group will not interact. However, this practice is now found in middle schools and, surprisingly, even in elementary schools. A consistent pattern persists with a majority of these younger bullies; they often have older sisters who engage in the practice. Although many of these younger bullies admit to learning about the practice from watching their older sisters, they claim that they have refined their skills through exposure to television shows designed to educate on the bullying topic on such channels as Disney and Nickelodeon. This is why Williams, a psychologist conducting an extensive study on ostracizing, states that the practice is difficult to extinguish. When educating some individuals on the negative impact of the behavior, the program often teaches and empowers perpetrators engaged in the action (Williams, Cheung, & Choi, 2000). Individuals prone to bullying behaviors tend to quickly apply information learned on different forms of harassment and its negative emotional impact to become more calculating at intimidation.

## BOYS PUNCH—GIRLS OSTRACIZE

It is now known that a simple act of ostracizing diminishes self-esteem and creates feelings of loss of control, sadness, and even anger (Williams, Cheung, & Choi, 2000). Even more damaging is the fact that individuals who have experienced being ostracized are more prone to going along with the behaviors of the majority even when they know that it is wrong, just to avoid experiencing the emotional impact of being ostracized again. This explains why so many healthy children who would typically not engage in bullying will join in the practice so as not to be excluded from the group.

Students who tend to have a greater chemical reaction to life's circumstances when repeatedly ostracized will take dramatic measures to put an end to the hurt that being alienated can cause. Some are capable of lashing out in attempts to physically or emotionally hurt those who have caused them such pain, while others have committed suicide to stop the pain (Wesselmann, Butler, Williams, & Pickett 2010). The Internet has leveled the playing field on bullying. You no longer have to be big and strong. You can be the anonymous bully hiding behind a screen name. The pain of being ostracized is real. MRIs indicated that the action triggers activity in the dorsal anterior cingulate cortex, a region of the brain associated with emotional and physical pain. For some individuals being ostracized is difficult to overcome. Individuals prone to anxiety or depression took significantly longer to recover from being ostracized. Repetitive exposure could trigger a range of emotional and physical problems.

Schools tend to focus on the overt practices of bullying and overlook the calculated practice of ostracizing because it is often perpetrated by some of the brightest female students. Some recent data on the lower levels of empathy of school-age children are revealing. The female brain is hardwired to be alerted to nonverbal cues. This sensitivity is essential to experiencing the feelings of empathy. It might be the lowering of empathy that is accounting for so many girls not being more sensitive to the impact their behaviors are having on their peers. It is time to recognize that exclusionary practices are just as severe as or even more harmful than being punched in the mouth by someone made of *frogs and snails and puppy-dog tails.*

The primary cause of bullying in both boys and girls is a lower tolerance for those whom they perceive as different. The amygdala has an increased reaction to differences, but for some individuals a more heightened response will be triggered, resulting in bullying behaviors. These heightened responses in boys often produce acts of aggression toward individuals they believe to be the most vulnerable. The increased reactions in girls often produce a desire to isolate those they perceive as different from their circle of friends. Ultimately, both boys and girls who experience a strong chemical reaction to individuals perceived to be different are at greater risk for inappropriate social behavior.

## AN EFFECTIVE STRATEGY
## FOR DECREASING BULLYING

One of the most effective ways to reduce a heightened response in the amygdala is by forcing it to focus on things individuals share in common. The amygdala is aroused by differences and eased by commonalities. When left to its own devices, the amygdala will be drawn to that which is the most familiar or common. This is why individuals tend to develop associations with others with whom they have things in common, and why in schools there are cliques between students and even adults. This is even more crucial for the teenage brain that is in a state of flux and seeks security in the presence of individuals he or she is compatible with. However, when under stress, the amygdala will become irritated by that which is different. Teachers need to intercede before the male or female bully has experienced a heightened response to those who are different from them.

Research has shown that having students learn that they share things in common, no matter how trivial, calms the amygdala and promotes healthier peer interactions. Teachers should engage students in games and activities that help them become aware that they all share things in common no matter how different they appear to be from one another. It is recommended that teachers focus on establishing a level of social comfort in the classroom prior to beginning any education on bullying. This reduces the tendency of students prone to bullying behaviors from utilizing the information to further advance harassing behaviors.

## THE BULLY BEHIND THE CURTAIN

It is important not to leave the topic on the transformation of bullying without making a few key points concerning the science of cyberbullying. The first aspect of cyberbullying that impacts human behavior is the element of anonymity. Researchers placed healthy normal adults in a dark padded room (utter invisibility) and through a specialized camera recorded behavior. Individuals confident that no one would know who they were displayed a sense of freedom that allowed them to cross the boundaries of social norms and decency (Gergen, Gergen, & Barton, 1973). When the brain perceives that behaviors are void of all accountability, it is prone to violate social norms and produce increased levels of affection and aggression (Kiesler, Siegel, & McGuire, 1984).

This begins to explain why a new behavioral phenomenon coined *toxic disinhibition* has manifested itself on the Internet. It is a level of disinhibition that seems to override the prefrontal cortex producing behaviors that often damage others or even oneself (Brotsky & Giles, 2007; Chau & Xu, 2007; Malamuth, Linz, & Yao, 2005). Online communication does not have the interpersonal triggers required to produce healthy interactions. The lack of face-to-face communication not only lowers empathy, but also alters how words are processed. When looking at words on a screen void of faces, we do not get the benefit of our orbitofrontal cortex producing emotional inhibition.

The human brain is also susceptible to participating in negative behavior when it perceives it to be prevalent. This is very common in riot situations. Individuals who normally would never participate get caught up in the pattern of behavior being modeled by the masses. The term *going viral* is the Internet version of mass hysteria. Many who participate with inciting comments are singled out to be the perpetrators; however, those who swing by the site to see what all the rave is about are also participants. The work of Dan Ariely at Duke University clearly illustrates that when you have increasing numbers of participants in an action, coupled with the belief that you cannot be caught, you have all the elements for mass participation (Gino, Ayal, & Ariely, 2009).

Cyberbullying is not only a teen problem. The moment adults rattle off an angry e-mail or smear a coworker they have joined the ranks of bullies. Research has shown that more adults participate in cyberbullying than adolescents. The Pew Research Center identifies that about 75 percent of American adults have witnessed online harassment and 40 percent have been victims of some form of cyberbullying (Duggan, 2014).

The difference between bullying and cyberbullying is that once posted to the web, the evidence of the mistreatment can always be found. To individuals who are emotionally fragile, the constant fear of others seeing the crucial act is much worse than being punched in the face. It is virtually impossible to erase something completely from cyberspace. The case of Ghyslain Raza is a clear example. In 2002, classmates posted a tape of an awkward adolescent trying out for a Star Wars skit in a school gala. It received 27 million views. A year later, the popular television show Family Guy did a parody of Raza's video skit. In 2006, someone posted the Raza's video with special Star Wars effects—12 million views. If that was not enough, someone was clever enough to insert Yoda into the video, so it seemed as if he was fighting Raza—2 million additional views. Other modifications of the video are occasionally posted. This student was so tormented by the initial posting that he was hospitalized for depression. He has to live with the fear of someone else viewing this video and forming an opinion about him for the rest of his life.

The feeling that everyone is laughing can create such a level of anxiety that vulnerable individuals will be at greater risk for depression, substance abuse, and suicide. A very popular student, Audrie Pott, at age 15 had a picture of her unconscious after allegedly being sexually assaulted spread across her high school. She later hanged herself. Numerous students have reported leaving their schools after an embarrassing picture or video of them spread across their high school. These students live in fear that the picture or video will resurface at the next school. Some students recounted having to move several times. In more extreme cases, parents reported having to uproot the family and move to a different state to give their child the opportunity at a normal high school experience.

Cyberbullying has elements that are devastating to the brain. The feeling that the humiliation cannot be erased impacts the sense of self. Remember, teens get their sense of self from others. The feeling that your most embarrassing moment will never be erased often leads to the brain encoding this perception of self into adulthood. The fact that so many people can witness your humiliation tends to produce a sense of paranoia and isolation, which can cause heightened anxiety and depression, and can trigger other emotional disorders. Cyberbullying is not like avoiding the bully at school. This bully is everywhere, can take on many forms, and even when not present, there is a feeling of impending doom.

## RECOMMENDATIONS

Once again, education is called on to step into the fray and help students cope with the evolution of bullying. However, the help must not be merely through policies and procedures that address how a student will be disciplined if caught engaging in the behavior. Schools must primarily do what they do best—educate. Most students and adults have a perception of what a bully looks and acts like in the real world. Most individuals who engage in cyberbullying do not perceive themselves as bullies. In this brave new world, a bully is anyone who engages in any *mean action* that upsets or offends someone else using electronic communication devices. In this context, no one can be absolved if the electronic action was not intended to upset or offend someone else. Students think that merely looking to see what everyone is laughing or jeering about is not intentional bullying. Character education and social skills programs have to become an integral part of effective anticyberbullying programs (Dygdon 1998; Lajoie, McLellan, & Seddon, 2001; Sanchez et al., 2001).

Research has shown that periodic student surveys that assess the prevalence of cyberbullying within the school environment seem to help students shift the issue in the brain from emotional to thoughtful (Greenya, 2005). By answering a few questions concerning key issues related to bullying, the brain is forced not only to process the emotional topic in the amygdala but also to consider it in the cortex that manages reasoning. This is achieved without lecturing, which can produce a negative emotional response.

Technology classes should teach appropriate online conduct. Adopting a code of conduct may be helpful. For example, a responsible online surfer refuses to pass on negative messages or even tell a joke that does harm to another online. A good standard for online behavior is the simple rule that if you would not do it face-to-face, you should not text, post, or pass it on. Schools cannot manage new problems by merely adding them to the list of behaviors to be punished—especially behaviors that are impacting education but are beyond the scope of many schools to adequately investigate.

The reality is that technology isn't good or evil by itself. We have a terrible track record on taking inventions that have the potential to help us and using them to harm others. The issue of teaching students ethical responsibility, as it relates to technological advances, is paramount in this day and age. However, the rate of technological innovations is happening so rapidly, and students do not have handbooks on how to use these advancements responsibly. With every innovation comes new opportunities and new perils. Cyberbullying should have sounded a clear warning that every technological advancement brings with it a new risk that could potentially transform child and adolescent behavior. Schools should become proactive in teaching technological responsibility and not wait until the next advancement becomes the next big issue.

# Diet and Education

12

XiXinXing/iStock/Thinkstock

## THIS CHAPTER

Changes in eating practices are altering a key region of the brain responsible
for healthy eating, sleeping, and addiction habits. Our eating and sleeping

practices have a direct correlation to the brain's ability to focus, fortify new information, and engage in higher-ordered thinking.

## SCHOOLS PLAY A KEY ROLE IN SHAPING EATING HABITS

In the same manner that bullying has been transformed through changes in technology and social media, something more fundamental has slowly been shifting right in front of us. It is noticed yet undetected. It is a significant issue with dire repercussions on the health and well-being of students, yet it is seldom acknowledged or addressed. Educators are becoming coconspirators in the problem, and yet their collective conscience is clear. Has no one stopped to notice that our students are getting physically bigger and maturing quicker? Has it gone undetected that health problems once reserved solely for adults, like adult-onset diabetes, are being experienced at younger and younger ages? The issue is linked to dietary practices, and schools consciously or unconsciously are playing a significant role.

Schools have the second largest influence on child and adolescent eating practices in the United States (Wardle & Cooke, 2008). However, due to budgetary concerns, many schools have contracted out the preparation of breakfast and lunch to companies that are for-profit. The outcome has been an increase of processed foods and diets that have excessive amounts of sugar and fat. The problem reaches far beyond obesity; it has to do with creating brain structures that are more susceptible to addiction and emotional illnesses, and are less capable of learning. It is time to face the fact that education plays a role in social learning. Educators cannot say we are teaching life lessons and preparing students for the future on one hand and protest against having to address matters that go beyond formal instruction. Children learn many things concerning life at school. Schools need to embrace education on eating, take control of developing good eating practices while at school, and help contribute to healthy eating lifestyles that are good for the human brain.

## THE NEW RISK FOR OBESITY

Humans need to eat to survive. That is why the human brain has two neurobiological mechanisms to govern food intake. The hypothalamus regulates when we need to eat to maintain health, and deep in the primitive brain strand the nucleus accumbens regulates the desire to eat. Since we require glucose and fat to survive, the nucleus accumbens secretes dopamine as a reward response to motivate the desire for foods containing sugar or fat.

This reward system ensures that we are motivated to overcome obstacles and even threats in search of food. Such a mechanism was crucial in more primitive times whenever food was scarce and when obtaining food was often dangerous. However, a problem arises when the desire to eat overrides the need to eat. The inability to forego rewarding foods consistently overrides the hypothalamus signals and over time begins to train the brain not to motivate food intake only when needed. This simple restructuring of the brain is a primary cause of obesity.

The nucleus accumbens came to the forefront in brain research related to its role in addiction. As mentioned earlier, it was commonly thought that most people develop an addiction by consistently overindulging in a substance that triggers dopamine in the nucleus accumbens. This excessive use causes a tolerance that forces them to continually need to consume more to get the same level of reward they initially felt. Later, it was discovered that a small segment of the population was already at a greater risk of addiction because they suffered from a phenomenon known as Reward Deficiency Syndrome (Stice, Yokum, Blum, & Bohon, 2010). As discussed in Chapter 7, these individuals appear to have fewer dopamine D2 receptors in the nucleus accumbens. The result is lower dopamine activity in everyday life. If these individuals consume a substance that triggers the dopamine D2, they will instantaneously have a stronger drive to consume higher levels. Because they are born with a built-in tolerance, they immediately will have to consume more to obtain the original high. It is likely that the 20 percent of the world who are genetically predisposed to becoming obese suffer from Reward Deficiency Syndrome. Others who become overweight are indulging in sweets or fats to the point of developing a tolerance forcing them to consume further (Volkow et al., 2001). In the past, those at risk of developing a tolerance represented a small segment of the population.

Changes over the last 50 years have caused the brain's system of need and desire to go terribly wrong. The crisis is evident in the dramatic increase in the number of obese people in the world. Some experts project that 2.6 billion people in the world are now overweight (Popkin, 2006). The growth has been exponential. For example, in Mexico in 1989, a very small proportion of adults were overweight and there were no overweight children. By 2004, 15 years later, 71 percent of the women and 65 percent of the men were overweight, with a level of diabetes that has begun to catch up with countries like the United States, which already had established long-standing poor dietary practices. The question must be asked, what has enabled the human brain to restructure so dramatically from a need to eat to a desire to eat in such a brief period of time?

Until 1940, it was commonly thought that obesity was primarily a result of genetic predisposition. Then in 1944, researcher Ancel Keys proved that you could take people who are not predisposed to eating disorders, dramatically change their intake habits, and produce behaviors commonly associated with individuals at risk for obesity (Keys, Brožek, Henschel, Mickelsen, & Taylor, 1950). Keys might have been the first to actually program compulsive eating and image disorders by reducing food intake by 50 percent, then allowing free access to unhealthy foods. The outcome was that the male participants in the study, after deprivation, overconsumed to gain back the weight they had lost. However, after getting back to normal body weight, they continued to overeat; they hoarded food and often woke up at odd hours just to devour more food. In a matter of months, not only did they become overweight, but they also began exhibiting body image issues: complaining their thighs were too fat and their butts were too big. Not liking themselves or their bodies, they felt ashamed. The conclusion was that obesity was not only the function of genetic predisposition but could be impacted by environment and behavior. Likewise, persistent short-term shifts in dietary practices could dramatically alter brain function to the point of promoting emotional disorders. This is a stark warning why starvation diets are not only ineffective but also dangerous to long-term eating practices.

Humans are hardwired due to centuries of evolutionary selection to seek high-calorie foods to keep us going through lean times. Food production and consumption were based primarily on survival needs. Once food production became a driving force in capitalism, for the first time we were motivated to apply our skills and knowledge to increase production and consumption. Producers no longer were happy with an economic market based on the need to eat but discovered that the ability to manipulate the desire to eat was far more profitable. Researchers like de Araujo discovered that merely increasing calorie intake intensifies dopamine levels in the nucleus accumbens (Ferreira, Tellez, Ren, Yeckel, & de Araujo, 2012). Findings like these began changing marketing strategies designed to alter behaviors concerning caloric intake. The research indicated that if the brain's system is consistently conditioned to consume more calories, it produces a tipping point—at which higher reward sensitivity erodes, resulting in a lowering of constraint.

What is more profitable than a population that has to eat? A population that desires to eat! That population will consume more and pay more, even if it kills them. By now it should be understandable why the constant emergence of fast-food chains outnumber any other form of restaurant growth. It should be noted that marketing experts and strategists are better students of brain science than the general population. Did it ever occur to people why fast-food chains offer larger meals at a cheaper price than if you purchase the items separately? Even if you say to yourself, "I will not consume all that food, but I am merely buying the meal deal to save the money," you have fallen prey to behavioral research. Wansink, the director of Food and Brand Laboratory at Cornell University, studied eating practices and marketing strategies and determined that individuals tend to consume 92 percent of whatever serving size is put in front of them (Wansink & Johnson, 2015). This simple strategy conditions the brain to eat more. The practice of grouping large portions of foods for less money is now standard practice in every fast-food restaurant in the United States.

The food items widely available at these chains, like cheeseburgers and milkshakes, are like super-foods regarding their caloric quantities. A rat study showed that after eating a high-fat and -sugar diet for 40 days, when deprived of high-fat human junk food, the rats would refuse to eat their healthy food for an average of 14 days (Johnson & Kenny, 2010). The study concluded that overconsumption of foods high in sugars and fats trigger the same brain circuitry activated in cocaine and heroin addiction. Even more frightening is the finding that overconsumption triggered addiction more rapidly and took longer for the brain's reward system to rebound when the behavior was terminated than cocaine or heroin. This means overconsumption of foods high in sugar and fat will begin to shift the brain to desire override. The high-fat and -sugar, junk food diet begins to reduce dopamine receptors very quickly.

For mice addicted to cocaine, it can take 2 days to regain normalized levels. The obese rats in the study conducted by Kenny and Johnson took 2 weeks to restore their baseline density of receptors. This indicates that the ramifications of poor dietary practices have a longer effect on the human brain. The odds of a healthy brain developing an addiction to an illegal substance are far more difficult than developing a food dependency. The simple difference is that you have to eat. All it will take is a dramatic shift to processed foods containing high quantities of sugars and fats. The problem is that this change in dietary practices has already occurred for many children and adolescents born into this fast-paced society. This shift of training the brain so early to consume high sugars and fats might explain why there are more obese people in developed countries than there are starving people in the world.

Stice and partners conducted a study using fMRI; they scanned the brains of adolescent girls while the young ladies viewed pictures of appetizing foods and imagined eating what they saw (Stice, Yokum, Bohon, Marti, & Smolen, 2010). The researchers then established a baseline of dopamine activity based on the sight of appetizing foods as well as their body mass index. Subjects were then followed for 1 year. The results were astounding. Girls who had lower dopamine activity were at greater risk for obesity. The next group at risk for becoming overweight was girls who had greater activation of dopamine in response to the sight of food. Stice found that as the girls' body weight climbed above optimal body mass index, their dopamine activation to the sight of food also increased. It appears that individuals who are not genetically predisposed to obesity but persist in an excessive intake of calories will create a catch-22 in response to the sight of desired foods. They see foods they crave and are motivated to eat, even if they are not hungry. If they consistently eat when they are not hungry, their craving at the sight of food increases. This begins to explain why millions of dollars in advertising are well worth the investment when coupled with strategies to increase food consumption. It should be noted that if individuals with intensifying dopamine responses to food continue to overconsume, the brain will eventually dampen the dopamine response, and the risk of obesity will be present without any preexisting genetic markers.

## ADDICTED TO NEGATIVE BEHAVIORS

I have focused only on the activation of dopamine from eating and how habits can restructure the brain. There is another added complication resulting from emotional trauma and stress. The nucleus accumbens secretes dopamine in recovery from physical or emotional pain. Many healthy coping behaviors trigger dopamine to help us deal with emotional upheaval and pain. However, since consumption of fatty or sugary foods directly triggers dopamine in the nucleus accumbens, an unexpected outcome has been that food consumption can become a form of self-medication. This is especially true for people who have not developed healthy coping mechanisms. The issue is that the greater abundance of these types of foods coupled with increasing stressors has increased the act of binge eating.

Binge eating is seldom about hunger. People who engage in binging claim that they are not hungry when they engage in the behavior. Binging is more about anesthetizing uncomfortable emotions using food. Many individuals who are healthy binge on their favorite sugary or fatty snack when stressed and do not realize it. Binge eating has become an acceptable method of dealing with stress in our society. A frequent scene on the television or in movies displays a woman who gets dumped and her friend pulls out a gallon of ice cream and some spoons to console her. High school surveys determined that most adolescents binge occasionally on their own and often with friends. The statistics say that up to 30 million individuals in the United States have diagnosable eating disorders (Hoek & van Hoeken, 2003; Hudson, Hiripi, Pope, & Kessler, 2007).

However, far more common is the practice of overeating to cope with stress, anxiety, and a range of emotional ills. In the previous edition of the *Diagnostic and Statistical Manual of Mental Disorders*, *DSM-IV* released in 1994, binge eating was not recognized as a disorder. But Harvard-affiliated researchers pushed for the binge-eating disorder to be included, noting that the incidence of binge eating is more than bulimia and anorexia combined, and it is probably an essential element in the epidemic of obesity. As a result, *DSM-5* released by the American Psychiatric Association in May 2013, now lists binge eating as a distinct disorder.

## THE NEED FOR INSTANT GRATIFICATION

An additional factor contributing to the sudden growth in obesity that is often overlooked is technological advancement. Primitive humans were hunter-gatherers, engaging in physical activity to survive. For centuries, we had to engage in physical activity to get through the day. However, technological advancements allow us to remain more sedentary, but what is even more significant is the fact that the human brain is becoming conditioned to instant gratification. The inventions of the automobile and the airplane continue to advance so we can get there faster. Television brought the world to our doorsteps, but computers, iPads, and cell phones bring the world to our fingertips. The average adolescent spends 4 to 6 hours on the Internet daily—however, merely an estimated 60 seconds per site.

The world of instant gratification has helped create a highly processed, fast-food world. It has long been established that the ability to delay gratification is an indicator of a healthy brain. However, environmental conditioning does cause even healthy brains to adapt. The technology revolution has created a side effect; immediate access to all forms of news and information has reduced our ability to delay gratification. The social side effect has been the search for instant solutions to problems better solved by discipline. For example, scientists at the University of California, San Francisco, reported in the journal *Cell Metabolism* that a small segment of the world's population can eat and not gain weight because their serotonin levels better manage calories once they are consumed (Srinivasan et al., 2008). Rather than concluding that the rest of the world needs to exercise caution, the scientists' response was that they hoped the research might develop a new form of drug that targets obesity without the need to suppress appetite. If you do not believe that our brains are becoming predisposed toward that which is easy and quick, then how else do you explain a billion dollar market dedicated to quick, effortless weight loss that can be achieved without the misery of exercise? Our cognitive brain is telling us that it is untrue, yet our desire for the quick fix still motivates us to buy it.

## DIETARY HABITS IMPACT ON BRAIN FUNCTIONING

There is a rich history of research studies that connect the brain's ability to learn to dietary habits. Research in the 1940s caused schools to begin free and reduced lunch programs for students who could not afford to purchase school lunches (Hinrichs, 2010). Later, a federal campaign based on the research conducted by the National Institute of Health identified the importance of eating a good breakfast and students' ability to perform academically during the first half of the school day (Levine, 2008). That campaign resulted in schools providing free and reduced breakfasts for students of economic need. However, current research has begun to identify that the brain's ability to perform optimally is based on *what* we eat (Gómez-Pinilla, 2008). Schools have been slow to reflect the current neuroscience findings on which foods help or hinder cognitive performance in school menus.

## RECOMMENDATIONS

The brain operates best when blood glucose is stable. Eating breakfast and snacking throughout the day are critical to stabilizing glucose levels. Rampersaud and colleagues' analysis of 22 students who eat breakfast found better memories, test scores, and attendance rates (Rampersaud, Pereira, Girard, Adams, & Metzl, 2005). Starch and fiber-rich foods such as whole grain bread raise glucose levels slowly. Wesnes and colleagues' study tested 64 students at hourly intervals and found that test scores declined each hour as glucose levels dropped; however, students with fiber-rich diets had a less severe decline (Ingwersen, Defeyter, Kennedy, Wesnes, & Scholey, 2007). Markus and Firk's study monitored 48 students prone to stress and found that high-carbohydrate meals dampen stress hormone reactions to math tasks in high-stress individuals (Firk & Markus, 2009). De Andraca and colleagues' study found that there is a correlation between iron deficiencies and speech deficits (Lozoff et al., 2003). Wurtman's study found that people who are anxious, depressed, stressed, or in pain are going to be drawn to sweets and fats because it temporarily elevates mood (Wurtman & Wurtman, 1989). Educational systems are aware of food's impact, and yet many of the foods served in school cause glucose levels to spike, producing a lethargic brain. Many of the meals are not balanced, causing reduced functioning for students susceptible to anxiety and stress.

The brain has many types of hardwired biases. For example, negative bias helps us become extremely cautious toward any change because it could harm us. I fear that the adapting brain, if the current trends persist, will develop an instant bias. Rather than facing the need to change, we eat, drink, and act merry while hoping for an instant cure before it is too late. We have turned the game of life into the biggest lottery in the world, chances of surviving without having to change how we eat and how much we exercise, 256,000,000 to 1.

Schools historically took an active role in teaching about food. Agriculture, home economics, and health classes provided guidance on food growth, food preparation, and healthy eating practices. Lessons on the impact of dietary practices on the body and the brain could easily be folded into the school health curriculum. However, due to budget cuts and a perceived lack of value of such classes, the primary education done concerning food in schools is modeling. What is served in the cafeteria, how much we see our peers eat, even the speed of consumption are influencing students' dietary habits. Almost nothing in our social climate has changed as much as food production and sale. Its impact has produced increasing medical costs that the nation is unable to pay. It is producing a generation of students at risk not only for obesity but also for increased drug addiction and emotional disorders. Increasing numbers of children and adolescents have already made the shift to a highly processed, fast-food diet and are experiencing the physical, emotional, and cognitive ramifications.

Schools must play a role in educating students on what is being done to their brains and equip them with the ability to make better decisions. A section in the social studies curriculum can teach students the strategies that fast-food chains, media, and food producers are engaged in. They seek to get you conditioned to eating more and more calories to the point that the sight of a rewarding treat triggers a desire to eat beyond need. Similarly, every related research finding on health is quickly employed as a marketing strategy by the large food companies to deceive your behavior. Researchers say that saturated fat is bad for you. The package covers blaze, *low in saturated fat*, hoping you do not notice it is loaded with sugar, high in sodium, and filled with preservatives. Advertisement agencies are aware that humans are now conditioned for instant gratification; these companies are confident that you will not become educated or take steps to make certain that you are not fooled.

Physical education classes should be playing a more significant role in health education for the 21st century. In addition to diet, physical education classes should help students realize that the human body was designed to move. Our student's lifestyle has many of them sitting in a car to school, sitting at school, sitting on the ride home, and then sitting in front of a computer or television screen. A simple rule should be adopted, if you have not engaged in at least 30 minutes of exercise a day, you are letting down your body and your brain.

Obesity is the result of a complex interplay among biological, behavioral, cultural, environmental, and economic factors. When it comes to complex social issues, a commonly heard mantra is, "Where do we begin?" In the case of the obesity epidemic, the answer is at the beginning—grade school. There are elementary schools that have begun to expose children to more fruits and vegetables. The early results have been expanded palates and more of these children requesting those types of foods at home. Simple steps can have a significant impact. These steps are worth taking because they protect the brains of the future.

The unseen risk is transforming the brains of students and contributing to addictive behaviors and increased emotional problems. Schools have always adjusted the curriculum to address social issues. A majority of public schools provide education on human sexuality, alcohol, and substance abuse. Schools facing issues related to the discrimination of subgroups have addressed the problems head-on through speakers, focus groups, and student counseling. How can schools turn a blind eye to an issue that impacts every student regardless of race, culture, and socio-economic status? The statistics reveal that the economic impact of poor eating habits on physical, emotional, and cognitive health will exceed that of smoking, alcohol, and substance abuse combined (Institute for Health Metrics and Evaluation, 2013). It is time to shine a light on the unseen risk and make students aware of this new serious threat.

# 13 Male and Female Brains

Wavebreakmedia Ltd/Thinkstock

## THIS CHAPTER

There might be no more fundamental way in which educators can better understand student social behavior than gaining insight into the male and female brain. This is a timely topic since so many education experts are promoting the idea of separating boys and girls to better design instruction to be more compatible with their distinct brain functions. It is important first to know what the distinctions between the male and female brain are and then what conclusions can be drawn from them.

## THE ROLE OF ESTROGEN

Until 8 weeks of life, every brain is female. A hormonal surge of either estrogen or testosterone makes the female and male brain, respectively. The surge of estrogen allows the brain to develop symmetrically. This is significant because language development requires the entire brain to act in concert. In addition, girls have a larger corpus callosum, which allows for more efficient communication between the left and right brain. Not only is the female brain more efficient going from the left to the right brain, but it is also blessed with specific glutamate receptors that allow for faster communication between neurons. These glutamate receptors are found in the region of the brain responsible for learning, enhancing focus, memory, and the ability to notice details (Boulware et al., 2005). This gives girls some distinct advantages in traditional classrooms that dispense information verbally and demand recall.

In addition, estrogen impacts social behaviors. Females are better able to read nonverbal cues because they are wired to make better eye contact, gaze at faces, and interpret what the other person is feeling. Girls also have a significantly larger orbitofrontal-to-amygdala ratio. By having the thinking part of the brain more connected to the emotional center of the brain, girls are better able to process their emotions without becoming impulsive. Although females can seem more indecisive, in reality they are processing problems from all sides. Girls' advanced communication skills are even reinforced chemically through a hormone called *oxytocin*. Oxytocin is the social bonding hormone that enables the building of trust and helps regulate stress. Girls get oxytocin released during conversations with close friends. That is why they can talk on the phone for hours; they are getting a chemical payoff. These differences in brain structure and chemical responses make girls more socially advanced earlier, better able to demonstrate empathy, and more prone to talking out problems.

## THE ROLE OF TESTOSTERONE

On the other hand, testosterone causes shrinkage of cells involved in communication, observation, and the control of emotions. Testosterone causes asymmetrical brain development, resulting in more activity in the left hemisphere. The left hemisphere of the brain processes logically, linearly, and visually. The male brain structure is better able to process visually in three dimensions, which enhances spatial reasoning associated with the development of math and science skills. Boys have the ability to focus long term on a single problem or challenge. The ability to concentrate on one thing coupled with a larger amygdala creates a brain designed to focus on competition; that is why boys can play a video game for hours attempting to beat their friend's high score. The brain's right hemisphere experiences greater automated embodied cognition experiences when processing language than the left hemisphere. As a result, boys require more active instruction to better integrate information and to compensate for lower embodied cognition experiences when processing language.

Testosterone, like estrogen, impacts social behavior. It can lower the ability to read nonverbal cues, feel empathy, and communicate. Several studies have shown that the higher the testosterone levels in utero between 12 to 18 weeks, the lower the ability to focus on nonverbal cues, bond, and socially interact appropriately. For example, Baron-Cohen and associates studied 38 children (24 male, 14 female) and found that the higher the fetal testosterone levels in the amniotic fluid during the first trimester, the poorer the child's social development by age 4. Also, the children with extremely high fetal testosterone levels consistently demonstrated a lack of empathy during follow-up observations at age 4 (Chapman et al., 2006). Another similar study found that children with the highest testosterone levels at 12 to 18 weeks in utero tended to focus on objects rather than the face of their caretaker during infancy (Lutchmaya, Baron-Cohen, & Raggatt, 2002). The trait of focusing on objects correlated with poor social skills at age 4. In addition to higher testosterone levels, boys have larger amygdalae accounting for increased aggression and sex drive. While girls have a higher level of involvement of the cerebral cortex during times of emotions, boys do not. This means that boy's emotional responses will be active rather than verbal.

## RECOMMENDATIONS

What conclusions should the education community draw from what we now know about the male and female brain? The first is that education should seek to be more interactive. It has been proven that both sexes learn faster through multisensory instruction. Brain-based instructional strategies have been found to be an effective method for girls to improve spatial reasoning, linear logic, and become more drawn to math and science. The same multisensory instructional strategies allow boys to improve language comprehension and memory and gain a greater appreciation for literature and the arts. The reality is that education should be modifying instruction to help all students, regardless of gender or cognitive deficiencies, overcome issues to succeed.

- For example, increase the use of manipulatives in language lessons for boys and in math lessons for girls.

The second conclusion that should be drawn is that school discipline needs to focus on the demonstration of what it is that the adults expect students to do rather than verbal directives. Girls are very capable of learning through observation, and boys require it. In addition, during times of arousal, the female voice causes a higher level of chemical activity in the human brain than the male voice. This means that talking through some incidents might trigger more impulsive behaviors by students who are more at risk. By adopting a discipline model that demonstrates desired behaviors, some incidents will be avoided and desired practices will be internalized quicker.

- For example, have boys role-play alternative methods of dealing with a conflict that can be employed rather than getting into physical altercations. It is practicing what to do rather than being told what to do that helps the male brain process expectations accurately.

The current movement to separate male and female education is being promoted primarily by educational institutions offering gender-based education programs. These institutions have a vested interest in manipulating the new research to support separate male and female education. However, it is important to note that some males share brain structures commonly associated with the female brain and some females share brain structures usually associated with the male brain (Baron-Cohen, Knickmeyer, & Belmonte, 2005). The research conducted by Billington and colleagues (2007) found that males who shared similar brain structures generally associated with the female brain demonstrated higher levels of empathy, intuition, and communication skills. On the other hand, some females who shared similar brain structures ordinarily associated with the male brain displayed higher spatial reasoning and lower empathy and communication skills (Billington et al., 2007). This means that making distinctions based on the gender of the student does not guarantee compatibility with an instructional model. The human brain learns new information by relating it to what it already knows and has been exposed to. *The hope of better male and female social relationships requires early and constant exposure to one another.* Many of the academic and behavioral distinctions between the male and female brain can be addressed through quality instruction and sound discipline. Separation and exclusion models have and will always prove problematic at the point of reintegration.

# 14

# The Subtle Influence of Bias

Susanne Dittrich/Fuse/Thinkstock

## THIS CHAPTER

Due to how the human brain functions, we all have biases. Implicit bias shapes our behaviors and attitudes as strongly as explicit bias. In some ways, implicit bias is more insidious because it is difficult to guard against and its impact is often the same as explicit bias. Awareness is the key to mitigating the impact of bias.

## IMPLICIT BIAS

Over time, most educators begin to know a lot about each student. Teachers begin to understand how students learn as well as their academic strengths and deficits. If teachers develop a relationship with a student or are merely observant, they can come to know many things about the child's background, likes, dislikes, social abilities, and even past traumatic events. Therefore, educators must become aware of how bias works in the human brain and how it can influence subconscious and even unconscious behavior. It would be virtually impossible for a teacher not to formulate strong opinions concerning students since the very nature of the vocation is to evaluate performance. Recent findings in neuroscience can aid educators to guard against the negative impact of bias and even learn how to develop some positive biases that could improve student performance.

Recent sophisticated assessment methods have established that people unwittingly hold an astounding assortment of stereotypical beliefs and attitudes about social groups: black and white, female and male, elderly and young, gay and straight, fat and thin. Although these implicit biases inhabit us, they can constantly vary depending on our own group membership and our everyday environments (Carpenter, 2008).

It is the nature of explicit bias that has placed our focus on the outrageous actions by extremists and that has led many to maintain that implicit bias is of secondary concern. However, hundreds of studies of implicit bias show that its effects can be equally insidious because it is far more widespread and often unrealized. In the past, it was thought that implicit bias did not impact human behavior. However, Russell H. Fazio of Ohio State University says that the data are incontrovertible that implicit bias influences our daily behavior (Fazio, 2014).

Implicit biases grow out of a normal process that enables learning. The human brain gains new understanding based on what it already knows. The brain associates new information with old and files related data together. Therefore, connections occur naturally due to the learning process. More important, the original function of the ability to naturally make associations was a product of the primitive brain to enable survival. Our basic survival requires us to be able to associate hazardous things with danger. The distinction between relationships held in the cognitive brain and those held in the primitive brain are significant. Connections held in the cognitive brain imply control over information, conscious awareness, and intentional behavior.

Associations held in the primitive brain indicate a lower level of control, awareness, and unintentional behaviors. The amygdala, a key player in the primitive brain, secretes chemicals when aroused that cut off interference from the cortex. This is a necessary feature since the amygdala is in charge of survival and, when threatened, does not want to compromise reaction time by the slower more deliberate process of the cortex. The negative outcome of this feature is that views held in the amygdala influence actions without our being able to cognitively control the reaction. The amygdala seizes control of our nonverbal behaviors to express emotion and to reflect strongly held implicit biases. The nonverbal behaviors include facial expressions, hand movements, body posture, and tone of voice. In addition, since the amygdala is a reaction system, it is likely to produce behaviors at any level of emotionality. Therefore, even dormant implicit biases will trigger a range of actions. To make sense of the world, the human brain puts things into groups, and the retrieval of certain data often causes unintentional associations. Without this most basic of abilities, we could not navigate the world around us. Since this is such a natural process, research has concluded that we all possess implicit bias.

Hence, some associations reside outside conscious understanding in our primitive brain. The problem arises when we form associations that contradict our intentions, beliefs, and values. For example, many minorities in the United States believe racial profiling to be wrong. However, after 9/11 when many of these individuals traveled by plane and saw an Arab, their minds automatically associated the person with a terrorist. This bias was understandable. Thousands of Americans had just spent a concentrated number of days viewing emotionally charged news on television associating a brutal act of terrorism to a group of people. Since this was such an emotional experience, it was stored in our amygdala. The amygdala is also the part of the primitive brain that is in charge of emotional memory. Therefore, even though the values of many of these minorities are vehemently opposed to any form of profiling, their emotional brain had already developed a bias that was opposed to their cognitive values and beliefs.

## THE EARLY FORMULATION OF BIAS

Most of our implicit biases are formed either before we can defend against them or by the patterns in our environment that are unavoidable.

Therefore, biases are formed by the little things we experience during our early development—the stories, comments, and even jokes people tell concerning a group of people. Other biases are a product of the saturation of information that is a product of today's instant media. Once a story breaks, you cannot avoid it. It is on the television, radio, Internet, and in the newspapers. Once a storyline presents a persistent pattern and is repeated over and over for an extended period of time, it is hard not to develop implicit biases. In addition, a person's environment often produces implicit biases. The nuances of a person's job begin to influence individuals over time. The workplace often produces some of the stronger implicit biases that humans develop.

## ENVIRONMENTS CAN PRODUCE BIASES

School environments can unwittingly help promote bias. Any disproportionate representation by any one group within the school settings will promote bias. For example, if students of Asian descent represent only 11 percent of the student population but 45 percent of the honors program, the brain will, over time, begin to associate Asians with the honors program. However, negative associations are far more harmful. For example, if black students represent 18 percent of the total student population but 66 percent of students in special education, then the brain will begin to associate black students with students with high needs.

The relevant question is, does implicit bias actually influence human behavior? The answer is yes. Some studies indicate that implicit association may be especially vulnerable to life situations requiring reflexive actions and snap judgments made by the amygdala. For example, a number of studies that asked whites and blacks to make a snap judgment about whether the person had a weapon or a harmless object in his or her hand, consistently found that both blacks and whites tend to mistake a harmless object, such as a cell phone or hand tool, for a gun if a black person held the object. The reflex or snap judgment made by the participants is understandable. We live in a society that continually portrays a higher rate of crime and violence by black males. Black and white students in schools where the rate of suspension of black students is disproportionately higher than that of students in the majority often claim that school personnel seem to assume the involvement of black students standing in the vicinity of any incident. This behavior is consistent regardless of the race of the school personnel.

## RECOMMENDATIONS

So what can be done to combat bias in schools? The following recommendations are offered:

*The first recommendation is simple*—no bad classes, no bad schools. Avoid allowing associations to be made by adults and students alike. Nothing can be more damaging than a student being associated with a slow class or a teacher with a bad school. When possible, districts should take active measures to avoid concentrating underperforming students at one site. In the same manner, schools should avoid developing classes for underperforming students to prevent the brain from making the easy association between certain individuals within a classroom to academic failure.

*The second recommendation* is to identify students with potential in any academic area from underperforming subpopulations for future acceptance in gifted programs. Once potential students are identified, actively prepare them to qualify and encourage them to enroll in advanced classes and the gifted program. This simple change in the gifted and advanced class's demographics will help develop a positive bias toward the students belonging to those subpopulations. School systems should also consider adding alternative screening instruments that are not based on traditional indicators for access into gifted programs, such as the Universal Nonverbal Intelligence Test (DeThorne & Schaefer, 2004). Having honors classes and a gifted program that represents the entire school population can combat long-standing perceptions concerning who can academically excel. If a student excels only in one academic area, allow that student to maximize his or her potential in that one area. Neuroscience has proven that the brain is prone to compensate for one deficit area by maximizing performance in another. The science also proves that the impact of many deficits can be reduced by maximizing the performance in any area of the brain. Therefore, teachers should be seeking to identify gifted abilities in all students, even those with cognitive deficits.

*The third recommendation* is for teachers to actively recruit students to become involved in extracurricular activities. It has been well established that students who play sports, participate in the band, or are involved in school clubs do better academically and socially. Many of the reasons are related to brain development, which was discussed earlier in this book. Aside from all the benefits participation in extracurricular activities has on the human brain, involvement in extracurricular activities also seems to reduce many negative biases held by teachers toward students and students toward the institution of school.

***The fourth recommendation*** is for teachers to promote climates conducive to change. Individuals coming from unstructured environments who have been exposed to stress and violence have the greatest problems adjusting to school. When they attend schools that work diligently in structuring and supervising the major transitions of the school day, their behaviors will become consistent with those of other students, thus preventing patterns that create bias from forming.

***The fifth recommendation*** is for teachers to be vigilant for any disproportionate patterns in their school environment. For example, teachers today are conditioned to constantly review student test performance. If there is a group of students who consistently underperform in comparison to their peers, it would be difficult not to develop a bias. Once you acknowledge the risk of a bias, you can take measures to prevent it from influencing attitudes and behaviors.

As humans, we might not be able to prevent biases from occurring, but we can diligently prevent them from being institutionalized. Negative biases profoundly influence what people see—they prevent us from seeing the greatness in many students. More tragic is the fact that biases influence how students perform and ultimately their perception of self.

# 15 Designing Replacement Behaviors

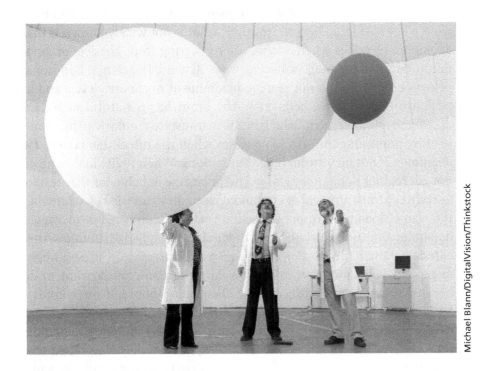

Michael Blann/DigitalVision/Thinkstock

## THIS CHAPTER

The human brain rewards consistent action through dopamine. It is this reward that motivates us to do mundane but significant tasks over and over again. Learning to design academic and behavioral interventions in a manner that the brain will reinforce the practice is the key to effective interventions.

## STRUGGLING STUDENTS OFTEN SUFFER FROM REWARD DEFICIT SYNDROME

This book has continually shown readers how to take abstract concepts and translate them into concrete actions. Instruction consists of layering actions designed to improve recall and comprehension of advanced concepts and promote higher-level thinking. Restoring the motivation to learn and the desire to behave requires translating the concept of success into concrete actions. This chapter explains the research that identifies why actions are the key to continually improving the structures and functions of the human brain. Humans are wired with a self-improvement method that is neither nebulous nor unobtainable. The brain is designed to improve through positive actions.

It is now widely accepted that dopamine in the nucleus accumbens plays a key role in addiction. However, what is not widely known is that dopamine responds whenever we are recovering from physical or emotional pain. Individuals suffering from Reward Deficiency Syndrome possess brains that do not secrete dopamine at normative levels and in response to normative behaviors. The brain has a natural desire for dopamine reinforcement, which needs to transpire regularly to maintain healthy brain function. An issue arises when the unconscious need for dopamine is not met through healthy actions. When individuals who do not get regular dopamine reinforcement engage in behavior that results in recovery from physical or emotional pain, they run the risk of craving this same dopamine response again. Void of healthy ways to trigger dopamine they unconsciously put themselves in high-risk situations that can cause them physical or emotional pain. Therefore, a person might engage in behaviors that he or she does not consciously want to do because they unconsciously desire a chemical response. If this sounds a lot like addiction, it is.

What distinguishes individuals with Reward Deficiency Syndrome from the majority of the population? Most individuals being raised in a structured household engage in daily practices that are taught, expected, and reinforced: waking up on schedule, getting ready for school or work, participating in meal customs, bedtime rituals, completing homework, having chores, keeping curfews. Once a healthy individual begins to engage in these practices consistently, over time the brain will reinforce these practices with dopamine. Therefore, most individuals engage in many healthy behaviors because they experience dopamine reinforcement. Once a dopamine response is consistent, extrinsic motivation is no longer needed. For example, many children are trained to make their bed in the morning. As adults, most maintain this behavior. Many adults often tell themselves that the practice is "stupid" because no one ever sees the bed but them, and it is actually a poor utilization of time and effort. Nevertheless, the next morning they awake and make the bed again. This is a clear indicator that the behavior is receiving dopamine reinforcement.

## INTERVENTIONS NEED DOPAMINE REINFORCEMENT

An abnormal dopamine response pattern complicates the ability to engage consistently in healthy behaviors. Most replacement behaviors taught by schools often do not trigger dopamine reinforcement (e.g., counting to 10 when angry). The chemical definition of *depression* is any life event that produces a dramatic shift in the brain's natural secretion patterns. This is why most crisis situations consistently produce some level of depression. Consider students who lack healthy dopamine response patterns and engage in high-risk behavior, such as kicking adults whenever angry. Since the behavior is a response to anger they are feeling, dopamine is activated to aid in their recovery from pain. The students are then taught to count to 10 when angry as a replacement behavior to kicking.

In reality, the alternative behavior has two unintended chemical outcomes. First, it diminishes the dopamine response the student consistently gains when engaging in the high-risk behavior. Although kicking is not a healthy practice, the dopamine-deprived child receives dopamine whenever he or she is recovering from a violent episode. Second, any period of abstaining from the negative practice results in depression because it causes a sudden shift in the brain's dopamine levels. The student, in reality, had learned a method to self-medicate. Once the student attempts not to engage in kicking, there is no dopamine recovery response. In other words, while the student is outwardly doing the desired behavior, inwardly he or she feels worse. This might explain why teachers commonly report that when troubled students refrain from engaging in habitual negative practices for any length of time, they seem tense and capable of escalating at any moment. This observation might be valid because when not engaging in habitual negative patterns, the student is experiencing escalating chemical instability. So is there no hope for the students with severe behavioral problems who require individualized interventions? The answer is that there is hope, but the response has to be prescriptive. The science behind behavioral change has determined that replacement behaviors cannot merely be what one does instead of established negative actions.

## NEGATIVE BIAS AND DISCIPLINE

Early discipline policies were highly influenced by negative bias. Research determined that our brains are designed to place greater emphasis on negative events than positive incidents. Individuals with difficult temperaments, shy and anxious temperaments, or who suffer from emotional disorders tend to be more prone to a higher level of negative bias. It should be noted that staff with any of the above-mentioned profiles are going to be more resistant to change because they are likely to view any change negatively. The result of negative bias on child rearing and discipline initially focused on the negative behavior and responded with some punitive action. In other words, the response to a negative action is with another negative action. When schools utilize this approach, it seems to be effective for a majority of the students; however, it is not effective with the students who chronically misbehave. This creates a catch-22—the more the student with chronic issues misbehaves, the more frequent the consequence; the more frequent the consequence, the more likely that the student with chronic issues misbehaves.

There are reasons the focus on the negative behavior and the punitive response does not work in curtailing chronic misbehavior. Merely identifying the wrong behavior when it occurs and punishing it does not teach the student what should be done instead of the poor behavior. Furthermore, a greater emphasis on punishment triggers distrust with this profile student. When a student who tends to violate social norms is put into an environment that is too punitive, he or she will experience *hostile attribution bias*. Hostile attribution bias is marked by temporary bouts of paranoia in which an individual misinterprets even benign actions as aggressive. When experiencing temporary paranoia, the student will become impulsive and even violent. This is why schools that implement a "get-tough" approach often see a reduction of targeted behaviors among the majority of students while experiencing an escalation in negative behaviors by the students they most seek to control.

## THE SHORTCOMINGS OF COUNSELING

The next evolution in school discipline on the surface looked more evolved, yet had the same mixed results as the punitive approach. Individuals who did not believe that consequences are effective sought to counsel students. The hope was that by helping them better understand why they did what they did, the students could learn how to control their behavior better. The issue with this approach is that students who tend to consistently violate rules are inclined to score high on the Machiavellian Index (Malterer, Lilienfeld, Neuman, & Newman, 2009). The Machiavellian Index rates how inclined an individual is to manipulate others to avoid consequences. These students, when interacting with a person in authority, experience activation in the dorsolateral prefrontal cortex, a region responsible for evaluating the threat of punishment. The constant activity in the dorsolateral prefrontal cortex when violating social norms and institutional rules helps these individuals be more skilled in manipulating others and avoiding consequences (Spitzer, Fischbacher, Herrnberger, Grön, & Fehr, 2007). With this profile student, the counseling approach is often manipulated. The student determines what the authority figure wants to hear and becomes skilled at feigning sincerity. However, counseling is effective with individuals whose issues are not as severe. Therefore, those who favor the counseling approach tend to focus on the times counseling proved effective.

## CONFIRMATION BIAS

It is important to note that the brain will focus on events in the environment that support existing beliefs and values. This is called *confirmation bias*. Research has clearly proven that individuals unintentionally miss events that challenge existing beliefs. On the other hand, confirmation bias ensures that events in the environment that support existing beliefs will not be missed. For example, if a teacher believes a student is prone to bad behavior, he or she is more likely to notice most violations. However, if a teacher believes a student is a model pupil, he or she is less likely to notice violations. Therefore, existing beliefs continually get validated and become even more entrenched. Existing staff biases often influence the elements of the discipline policy put in place, which can result in flawed planning and inconsistency. In addition, bias impacts every staff person's ability to monitor student behaviors accurately.

The current model of school discipline being supported nationally is to teach replacement behaviors and reinforce them when demonstrated. The recent trend of teaching replacement behaviors and reinforcing them seems on the surface to be aligned with current brain research. Yet a closer look reveals that some critical aspects of brain research are being overlooked. As a result, the approach is experiencing results similar to discipline models that have failed in the past. One difficulty with how replacement behaviors are implemented is related to how they are taught. A student does a negative behavior and is taught an alternative practice that he or she should do when faced with a similar situation in the future. However, when something is learned that does not hold emotional value, it is stored in the cortex. When an individual is agitated, the amygdala releases chemicals that slow or even cut off information held in the cortex. During episodes of arousal, the student does not have access to the replacement behavior learned.

## NEUROSCIENTIFIC APPROACH TO REPLACEMENT BEHAVIORS

The recommended approach based on the latest brain research is to teach replacement behaviors so that they can be practiced with regularity while the student is calm. Asking a student to engage in an alternative practice only when they are aroused is not only unfair but also irrational. The student never practices the behavior when he or she is most capable of being successful—when calm. Also, the replacement behavior is not accessible during periods of arousal because it is held in the part of the brain that is not accessible during a crisis. The amygdala must value alternative behaviors for it to be reinforced by dopamine. Therefore, the design for successfully establishing replacement behaviors must meet the elements found in the research that promote the emotional value and chemical reinforcement.

The following example provides a quick review of how a teacher can establish a replacement behavior that meets all the steps identified in the science to help trigger dopamine.

*Mrs. Reddick's ninth-grade class has several students who become easily overwhelmed when facing small problems at school. Therefore, Mrs. Reddick introduces a problem-solving process and informs students that they can use this approach when solving academic and personal problems. She carefully sets up academic and real-life scenarios weekly for the students to consistently practice the problem-solving process. The teacher consistently ties the problem-solving method to one of the values of the amygdala by telling the students that using the process will make them more successful in life. Also, she prompts the student to use the problem-solving method by simply pointing her index finger to her head. She selected the gesture because people use it to remind others to think, but in this case it is also used to trigger motivation. Occasionally when the class or an individual is successful in using the*

> *problem-solving method, Mrs. Reddick rewards the class or student to help promote dopamine. Throughout the school year when students are having problems, Mrs. Reddick points at her head reminding them to think through the problem rather than act impulsively.*

In this example, Mrs. Reddick meets all the elements of designing a replacement behavior that is likely to be reinforced by the brain: She created an action, associated it with a value of the amygdala, used a gesture to trigger the behavior, established times to consistently practice the process, and randomly rewarded the behavior when students were successful.

The most difficult part of this approach is that educators are conditioned to focus on the negative behavior and are not trained to design replacement behaviors that can be practiced consistently while the student is calm. Treatment determined a long time ago that recovery is not linear. For example, resiliency research indicates that promoting specific protective factors will diminish presenting problems even if there is no direct correlation. In this case, protective factors are the skills identified in resiliency research that help students overcome presenting issues. This seems counterintuitive to most educators. If a student displays anger as an issue, teachers believe that the replacement behavior must be an anger management strategy the student is to do in times of crisis. However, research does not support that position. This approach allows educators to embed protective factors into daily class rituals, allowing students increased opportunities to master the skill and the brain to reinforce it. The key is to design the protective factors in a manner that the brain will reinforce the practice.

The following is a simplified approach to designing replacement behaviors that reduce presenting problems through actions. The goal is that the replacement behaviors are actions that trigger dopamine response.

## DESIGNING REPLACEMENT BEHAVIORS

Research has identified five key elements that should be in place for a replacement behavior to become a long-term intrinsic habit.

### Design in the Form of an Action

The first element is to design the replacement behaviors in the form of an action that is carried out in a sequential manner. An action completed in a sequential order aids the learning process. The hippocampus, where learning begins, is drawn to repetitive actions that follow a consistent order. A good example of this is how soldiers and athletes train. They follow a prescriptive training pattern in which they repeat a process over and over in the same exact order, hoping that they will be able to perform the action when under duress. Another advantage is that sequential actions become valuable to the hippocampus, increasing the probability that it will be held in the amygdala as well.

### Align to the Amygdala

The second element of a replacement behavior is that the amygdala must value it. It has been stated that the amygdala is wired to possess three values: the need to be safe, wanted, and successful. If a replacement behavior is consistently aligned to one of these values, it increases the probability that it will be held in the amygdala. This is important because, when individuals are aroused and need to demonstrate the alternative behavior, it will be accessible. This is because it is the amygdala rather than the cortex that is engaged during periods of arousal. It should be noted that when designing interventions for chronic offenders, it is best to align it to the value of success.

### Utilize a Cue

The third element is to utilize a cue to trigger the behavior. The cue can be a visual symbol or a gesture. Once an action is rewarded, the anticipation of doing the action occurs in the nucleus accumbens. However, when a symbol is associated with an action that is rewarded, it can trigger another form of dopamine reinforcement in the medial prefrontal cortex (MPFC). This is why the sight of something we have found desirable triggers motivation (Peterson, 2005).

In addition, the value of a visual symbol or a gesture is rooted in primitive communication patterns that existed prior to the inception of language. The amygdala is hardwired to focus on visual cues and gestures at all times. This is because visual cues and gestures were at one time the primary means of communication. This primitive system is still operative, even though we communicate primarily through language. Many times the influence of visuals and gestures occurs subconsciously or unconsciously. Observe individuals attempting to express something that is important, and their hands will naturally gesture, supporting what they are saying. The importance of having a visual symbol or a gesture to trigger a behavior is already demonstrated as a strategy to communicate to students who tend to become agitated. When a student is agitated, language often increases chemical instability. This explains why one of the strategies found to be most effective with students with severe autism is visual symbols or gestures to trigger learned behaviors. One of the features of severe autism is chemical instability that produces constant periods of irritation. Language can often increase the level of irritation while symbols and gestures are naturally focused on by the amygdala and are found to be comforting over time.

## Practice Consistently

The fourth element is that the replacement behavior must be practiced consistently. This explains why so many well-designed interventions fail. The length of time that is required for a new behavior to become a habit is in direct proportion to the student's level of emotional health. Therefore, the more pronounced the student's issue, the longer the practice must be in place before it is reinforced by dopamine. Teachers subconsciously establish the length of time change should occur based on the conduct of the majority of students. Once the majority of students master something, a teacher is naturally prone to think that a sufficient amount of time has taken place. The tendency at this point is to look for a new alternative behavior.

The teacher's conduct is based on how the brain learns. As discussed in the previous chapter, bias is developed by two things consistently being linked together in the environment. Once the linkage is established, the brain will make the association whenever one of the elements is recognized. For example, if black students represent only 10 percent of the student population and 50 percent of suspensions, then teachers will eventually connect black students to misbehaviors resulting in suspension. These types of biases develop over time regardless of personal values. Teachers determine daily the pace of learning based on when the majority of students understand the material. It is only logical that this same bias impacts behavioral interventions. The teacher applies the same bias of how long change should take that has been internalized by constant observation of students over the years. This bias occurs even if the teacher is aware that all students are not the same. This is where teachers have to fight the urge to continuously attempt new behavioral interventions if the current one is not quickly successful.

A consistent finding among high-risk students is that they are slow to adapt. Schools dedicate inordinate amounts of time to designing behavioral interventions for this population and then give up on them far too quickly. Teachers subconsciously expect the change to take the amount of time it takes for the majority of students to show improvement. As a result, schools ask the students who are the least capable of adapting to change, to make the most changes. The reason they are required to make the most changes is because they are asked to comply with a new plan each time the old plan does not produce instant improvements.

## Reward

The fifth element is reward. This element has been so misunderstood and poorly executed that many educators automatically reject it. Students who don't secrete dopamine within a normative range often need an embodied cognition experience to help activate the brain's reward response. However, reward in this case must meet the definition found in the research. There are certain accepted forms of extrinsic reward that help trigger dopamine.

One form of extrinsic reward that can help trigger dopamine is any reinforcer that is valued by the community. An example of this type of reinforcement is easily found in the realm of sports. Many football teams place stickers on the back of player helmets that signify a major accomplishment such as causing a fumble, throwing a touchdown pass, intercepting a significant pass, or running for an important touchdown. Every player on the team knows the importance of these symbols and how rare they are to obtain. These stickers become a driving motivator for players. The stickers have no monetary value, very few people outside the team understand their importance, but for team members it is a significant reward. The human brain is designed to attach emotional value to any object that is elevated by members of its community. This is why ancient tribes often had a symbol of power held only by the leader. This explains how street gangs can get someone to die for a color. Many firms have trophies that are held in the offices of the top performers, and educated mature people covet this symbol. It is not the value of the object; it is the importance the item represents to the community

Another form of extrinsic reward that tends to be reinforced by dopamine is anything valued by the giver. It is important to note that it does not have to be valued by the receiver. Research on nonverbal cues indicates that when someone gives a tangible symbol of recognition that is heartfelt, it is more likely to motivate the other party than an extravagant gift. The science supporting this is rooted in how the brain is designed to interpret nonverbal cues. Everything that is felt by the giver is subconsciously and unconsciously represented in his or her face, posture, hand movement, and tone of voice. The amygdala is hardwired to monitor nonverbal cues and draw emotional meaning. It is these nonverbal indicators that convey the importance of what is given. In this scenario, it is not what you give but how you give it. This explains why parents cherish the gifts that their children take the time to make, and why married people love the gifts that represent thoughtfulness and caring in selection from their spouse. On the other hand, it also explains the disappointment felt in receiving an extravagant gift that the spouse had an administrative assistant select because he or she was too busy.

A more recently discovered reward model was revealed by research on video games. Video games showed the ability to motivate a player past repeated failures by providing immediate positive sensory reinforcement for each positive action that would improve future success when playing the game. Research conducted by Tom Chatfield (2010) determined that many video games incorporate how the brain rewards behaviors through dopamine. The science behind video games has developed a mathematical model that predicts dopamine reinforcement by incorporating certain elements in each game. The elements identified to trigger dopamine are tasks that create a balance between level of difficulty and ease, break long-term goals down into clusters of short-term goals, reinforce effort, reward successful actions, and provide unexpected rewards and novel challenges as tasks become more difficult (Chatfield, 2010).

All these forms of extrinsic rewards require the element of surprise or anticipation to help trigger the desired dopamine response. Random reinforcement seems to secrete dopamine more than scheduled reinforcement. The brain adapts quickly to scheduled reinforcement, and it becomes a mere formality. The expectation over time results in the loss of a dopamine response. This is why many reinforcement programs in schools often lose their value. Staff members become unmotivated to give the reinforcers, and students become apathetic to receive them. Anticipation for many individuals is better than what is actually received. Humans are the only creatures on Earth who can play out scenarios in their mind. When predicting what will likely occur, we tend to exaggerate the impact of change.

The tendency to dramatize the impact of change is called *impact bias*. A common Christmas scenario can clearly illustrate this point. As a child, you loved Christmas. Every year you began to become excited the day after Thanksgiving. Each day closer to Christmas, the anticipation builds. You told Santa what you wanted and found ways to leave clever hints around the house for your parents. You yelled out how great that special toy you wanted was each time it came on the television. On Christmas Eve, you could barely get to sleep. You knew the next day your life was about to change. By 5:00 a.m., you were awake and attempted to make as much noise as possible so your parents would wake up. Then the moment finally came, your tore open packages, and finally received the toy that you knew would change the quality of your life forever. By Christmas afternoon, your mother looks at you and says, "What's the matter?" You say, "I'm bored." She says, "Why aren't you playing with your new toy?" You say, "I did, but I am already bored with it." The process of anticipation builds dopamine response. This is why humans are designed to get continually excited by certain events even after repeated disappointments. There is no magical gift; the wonder for the brain is in the anticipation. This is another reason reward programs in many educational settings fail. There is not enough investment to build anticipation.

There is no inherent problem with reward. The problem is that many educators do not understand how it can help the human brain trigger dopamine. The shortcomings are often related to the lack of investment by the adults. When there is a lack of investment from the adult role models, regardless of the reward, it cannot become valued by the community, valued by the giver, or anticipated. Schools also become too predictive in scheduling rewards, and they lose the element of surprise.

To summarize, these are the five elements for establishing a replacement behavior that is likely to be reinforced by the brain.

1. Design the replacement behavior in the form of an action that is carried out in a sequential manner.

2. Associate a replacement behavior with one of the three values of the amygdala.

3. Utilize a cue to trigger the replacement behavior.

4. Practice the replacement behavior consistently.

5. Reward the replacement behavior.

   – The reward must be valued by the community or the giver.
   – The reward must maintain a level of anticipation.

## CONSIDER REPLACEMENT BEHAVIORS THAT ARE PROTECTIVE FACTORS

Resiliency theory is rooted in a rich body of longitudinal research studies conducted all over the world. The studies tracked large cohorts to determine what caused poor life outcomes. The conclusion was that specific risk factors are associated with poor life outcomes. The studies concluded that it was not which risk factor one possessed but how many. During these studies, a resilient population emerged. The resilient population comprises individuals who are at high risk for poor life outcomes but somehow experienced successful life results. In studying these individuals, it was determined that they possessed a sufficient number of protective factors to offset the risk in their lives. The presence of these protective factors seems to reduce the negative impact of presenting problems.

Therefore, it is only logical that schools not waste time assessing what interventions to consider when attempting to curtail negative behaviors. Rather stand firmly on the findings of one of the largest bodies of research that has already identified ways of reducing chronic negative problems. The following is a list of protective factors found in the research that can be easily promoted within the school setting (Vance & Sanchez, 1998):

- Problem-solving skills at school age
- Ability to function as a good student
- Good reader
- Perceived competencies
- Involved in extracurricular activities
- Ability to get along with other children
- Ability to get along with most adults
- Considered likable by most people
- Thought to have a good sense of humor by most people
- Child demonstrates empathy
- Support from an adult at school
- Support for child from friends
- Adolescent feels confident that life events are under his or her control
- Adolescent has positive and realistic expectations for the future
- Adolescent actively plans for the future
- Female teenager is independent-minded

The following model lesson illustrates how a teacher can design a protective factor in a manner that it can be consistently practiced in the classroom while students are calm.

# CHAPTER 15 SUPPLEMENT TO DESIGNING REPLACEMENT BEHAVIORS

Wasja/iStock/Thinkstock

The protective factor selected in this lesson addresses the presenting problem of numerous students in the classroom. This example demonstrates how a protective factor can be consistently practiced in the classroom. Later in the chapter, information is provided on how the protective factor can be promoted in a manner that the brain will likely reinforce the new behavior.

## PRESENTING PROBLEM

A class has 30 students. Seven students consistently fail to demonstrate appropriate social skills. They seem unable to get along with students who are not from their neighborhood and who do not share the same interests and points of views. When upset, they tend to overreact to benign comments made by their peers. Many classroom incidents that occur stem from their overreaction. The outcome is a classroom with too many incidents of verbal conflicts, physical altercations, and loss of instructional time. The approach covered in this chapter is preventive in nature. The goal is to establish a classroom climate that prevents crisis. Many of the most severe behaviors in a classroom occur because there was insufficient investment in preventative strategies. Remember, poor classroom management manages a crisis only when it occurs, but effective classroom management prevents behavioral incidents from ever occurring. Improving students' social comfort with each other as well as social skills has been found to reduce bullying and verbal and physical altercations, as well as racial and cultural tensions.

## HOW WILL THE PROTECTIVE FACTOR BE PROMOTED?

The teacher has decided to promote the protective factor as a classroom strategy. There are many advantages to a classroom strategy rather than an individual intervention. A classroom strategy prevents any student from being singled out. In addition, classroom strategies advance the health of all students when they promote protective factors. Classroom strategies lend themselves more easily to regular practice times while students are calm.

## PROTECTIVE FACTOR SELECTED: THE ABILITY TO GET ALONG WITH PEERS (SOCIAL SKILLS)

The ability to get along with peers is a protective factor that is usually demonstrated early in life and remains consistent. However, a child or adolescent can develop this protective factor later in life. A student has likely gained this protective factor when he or she can consistently get along with peers across multiple settings. This protective factor should be consistently demonstrated for a period of 2 years for it to be considered as internalized. Getting along with peers is best denoted by the ability to tolerate students from different backgrounds, cultures, and socioeconomic status.

## LESSON GOALS

- Learn the role social skills play in life success.
- Learn to identify and properly interpret nonverbal cues to respond appropriately in social situations.
- Learn concrete skills that improve likeability.

The following module is for Grades 9–12; however, it can successfully be used in middle school grades. ***Teacher instructions are in bold italics.***

## HOW TO BE MORE SUCCESSFUL

*Although this is a social skills lesson, the term social skills is not utilized. Students with the most severe emotional disorders are not motivated to get along but are still driven to be successful. Also, at-risk students often resent the term social skills training because it implies that they lack social skills. Many of these students believe that when they want to get along with people, they can. The issue is that success in life requires the ability to get along with people who might not be similar to you. In addition, people who lack social skills often attract others who have similar issues. This prevents the student from developing a healthy support network. In extreme cases, the lack of social skills can lead to rejection and ultimately a loss of desire to get along with others. Perhaps the greatest reason to promote social skills is because of the benefits they have on brain function and learning.*

### Pick the People Who Are Meeting for the First Time

*The teacher will show students the following pictures and have them select the people who are meeting for the first time. The goal of this exercise is to help students realize the significant role external expressions have on social interaction. If students can identify them for themselves, then they will be better able to accept the fact that their external expressions need to align with their social goals.*

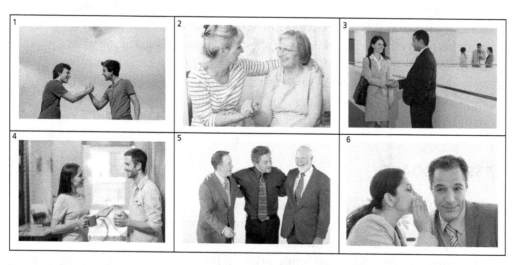

From top left: hjalmeida/iStock/Thinkstock; BakiBG/iStock/Thinkstock; Moodboard/ moodboard/Thinkstock; g-stockstudio/iStock/Thinkstock; Jupiterimages/ PHOTOS.com/Thinkstock; Wavebreakmedia/iStock/Thinkstock

*Most students should select Picture 3. Once they select Picture 3, the teacher can lead students into a discussion to help them better understand how their brains are designed to make that selection.*

### What Helps Us Pick the Correct People Just by Seeing Them?

- Our brains have a little almond-shaped region called the amygdala that helps us understand others. This is a good place to incorporate an embodied cognition strategy. Provide an actual almond that the students can see and touch. Then have the students make the shape of an almond with their hand to help recall the name of the amygdala. Show students a picture of where the amygdala is located in the human brain.
- The amygdala's primary job is your survival.
- The amygdala reads facial expressions.
- The amygdala reads body language.
- The amygdala interprets tone of voice.

### Why Do You Think the Amygdala Reads People?

- Survival
- How does reading people protect you?
- Can we all agree that we read people all the time?

*It is important to help students relate to how projecting and interpreting nonverbal cues plays an important role in social interaction.*

1. It is the reason we can look at our parents and know if they are upset.

2. Because reading nonverbal cues is related to survival, people have gotten into conflict just because of the way someone looks at them or the tone that they said something.

3. **Key point:** When you are upset, the brain becomes even more sensitive to nonverbal cues and tends to overreact.

4. Our nonverbal cues determine people's opinions about us and how they treat us.

## What Happens When You See a Person for the First Time?

- Look at the following people.

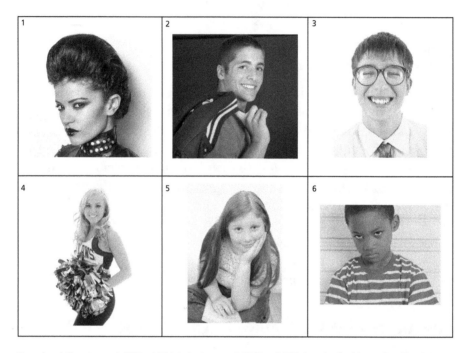

From top left: patronestaff/iStock/Thinkstock; spepple22/iStock/Thinkstock; shadrin_andrey/iStock/Thinkstock; Brian McEntire/iStock/Thinkstock; Moodboard/ moodboard/Thinkstock; Digital Vision/Photodisc/Thinkstock

- Did you think things about each of these people just by looking at them?
- We all form strong opinions about people in the first 30 seconds of meeting them.
- This means people formulate opinions about you in the first 30 seconds of meeting you.
- Have students write down the opinion they had about Pictures 3, 4, and 6. Then poll responses to see how many had similar perceptions.

  – What opinion do you think people formulate about you? Lead students into a discussion that helps them identify what their outward appearance and attitude are communicating to others. Ask students if they like the nonverbal message they are communicating. Then ask students what they think they could do to change their external appearances if they wanted more people to look at them for the first time and want to talk to them.

### Two Words You Need to Know

*These two vocabulary words are important in the field of neuroscience. The emotions we are truly feeling often are expressed subconsciously to others at all times. Strong emotional experiences are conscious and you are more aware of them.*

- Conscious—Aware of what you are thinking
- Subconscious—You think it, but you are not aware of it

***This is a good place to incorporate embodied cognition strategies to help recall and comprehension. See the following examples:***

- Utilize a picture to represent each word:

Zoonar RF/ Zoonar/Thinkstock

- Utilize movement:

champja/iStock/Thinkstock

Thinkstock Images/Stockbyte/ Thinkstock

### When We See People for the First Time

- The strong opinions about them will be conscious.

  - You know you are thinking it.

    o *She is beautiful!*
    o *He looks mean!*

- There are a lot of other opinions that are subconscious.

  - You don't know you thought it, but you did.
  - People you don't perceive you have really noticed, you have formulated a subconscious opinion about.

### Why Do You Think the Brain Makes Strong Personalities Consciously Stand Out?

- Survival
- You notice those you are attracted to.
- You are alerted to anyone who appears threatening to you.

### A Social Experiment Done With Different Groups of People

- It was done over 40 times.
- It was done in over 40 different states.
- People watched a 30-second video clip of a person they had never met.

  - Then they filled out a detailed questionnaire about the person.
  - Things they did not know, they guessed the answers.

- They also asked people who knew the person to fill out the same questionnaire about the person.
- In every place they did this experiment, the findings were the same:

  - People who saw the person for just 30 seconds on a video and people who saw the person on a regular basis answered most of the questions the same.

(Ambady & Rosenthal, 1992)

### What Does This Mean?

- Most people who see someone think the same things about them. Have the students recall how they shared opinions concerning the pictures they saw earlier.

  - *Perceptions Are Reality* (What you think, you believe to be true.)
  - What you think about someone determines how you will treat them.

### Let's Do a Quick Activity *(This activity is to help students experience that if people treat you based on how they perceive you, it will impact how you feel and act.)*

- The activity will let you see that what people think about you determines:

  - How they treat you
  - How you feel about yourself

### Rules for Activity

*Headbands will need to be created ahead of time for this activity. Generate a list of traits that include varying degrees of positive and negative traits, such as pretty, stylish, funny, angry, class clown, scary, mean, popular, sickly, rich, poor, and so on. Have 50 percent of the traits be positive and 50 percent of them be negative. Each headband will have one of the traits written on it. The headbands can be made with heavy paper or regular paper that is laminated. Take 3-inch wide by 8-inch long strips of paper and type one word in bold extra-large print centered on the middle of the strip. Cut holes at both ends just large enough to insert elastic string through and knot at each end so that a headband has been created. See example below:*

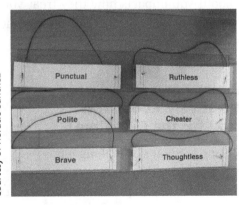

Courtesy of Horacio Sanchez

- I will pass out headbands face down on the desk in front of you.
- Do not touch them until instructed.
- When you are told to put them on, you must do it without seeing what is on your headband.
- You cannot read anyone's headband to them.
- When instructed, everyone will get up and socialize.
- You must treat each person in the room like you would if what their headband says about them is the truth.

## Guidelines for Running Activity

- Make sure students take rules seriously.
- Have 50 percent of headbands with positive personality traits and the other 50 percent with negative personality traits.
- Look for the following indicators to let you know that the exercise is complete:

  - *The students wearing headbands with negative personality traits have gathered around each other and remained together.*
  - *People are being emotionally impacted by how they are being treated.*

- Teachers should note that this exercise often causes some students to experience the emotions associated with what is on their headbands. Therefore, it is important to allow time to process the exercise and to help students see how they treat one another can cause emotional harm. It is important that students realize after this experience that facial expressions, posture, and tone of voice, as well as how you dress make people think certain things about you. What they think about you impacts how they treat you. How they treat you impacts not only how you will feel, but also how you will think about yourself.

## What Nonverbal Cue Makes
## People Think Positively About You
## When Seeing You for the First Time?

- The number one predictor of making a positive impression is if the person smiles when meeting you.
- The people identified in the pictures below are very different from you.

  - Even so, your amygdala should not be bothered because they are smiling.

From top left: Fuse/Thinkstock; AntonioGuillem/iStock/Thinkstock; Fuse/iStock/Thinkstock; ElNariz/iStock/Thinkstock; Milan Lipowski/iStock/Thinkstock; szefei/iStock/Thinkstock

## What Happens to the Amygdala When You Meet Someone New?

1. The amygdala gets alerted.
   - That means it can overreact.
2. The amygdala reacts less to faces that look like your own.
3. The amygdala reacts less to faces that don't look like yours when they are smiling.

## Skills for Being More Successful

*Skill 1: Smile*

- When you meet new people, a smile will help others want to interact with you.
- However, in more dangerous environments, smiling can place someone at risk.
  - For example, prison
- Individuals coming from more dangerous environments must learn to change their behavior when not in danger.
  - The inability to smile limits success.
- For example, lowers chances of being hired for a job, liked by peers, and being promoted.

### Skill 2: Greet

- Greetings usually contain two components: the spoken word and touch.

  - Anthropologists believe that touch is important because primitive humans used touch to identify danger and communicate safety. Neuroscientist now know that touch does far more than communicate danger and safety. Our sense of touch is directly linked to our emotions and, as a result, acts like social glue to bind people together. Touch helps the brain develop feelings of trust and cooperation quicker. Therefore, it is not surprising that individuals use handshakes, high fives, fist bumps, and even pats on the back when greeting someone for the first time or when reconnecting with a friend.
  - Anthropologists believe that primitive humans merely added words to the already established nonverbal social greeting of touch. The fact that we use common phrases when we greet each other is because the amygdala is drawn to familiarity, and if what we said when greeting each other was always different, it would make us anxious.

### Skill 3: Connect

- Once you have greeted someone during the conversation, it is important to then find out something you both have in common.

  - The amygdala is calmed whenever it finds out you share something in common with someone else.
  - Because the amygdala is in charge of your emotions, keeping it calm is important.
  - It is especially important when meeting someone for the first time because the amygdala is on alert around strangers.

Let's do an activity that will let you experience how sharing something in common with someone else makes the amygdala happy.

### Activity

- ***For the following activity, PowerPoint slides will need to be created that include pictures of items students may like and share in common with their peers. The teacher presents a picture on the screen (examples of pictures and headings are provided below) and communicates the following steps.***

  - If you like the item represented by the picture, stand.
  - When you stand, look around and high-five at least one other person who is standing.

- Each time you stand, look for a different person to high-five.
  - After the activity, I will give you a form with the pictures identified in the activity. Put your name on the top of the form. Circle each picture of the things you liked and hand it in. ***Utilize the information from the forms to place students in future group assignments based on things they share in common. Skillfully group students who do not socially interact regularly with one another to maintain a high level of social comfort in the classroom. It is highly recommended that the symbols used in the exercise be displayed at each table when grouping students to remind them of the initial activity and how they felt while doing it.***

| | | |
|---|---|---|
| Stand if you like pizza | Stand if you like music | Stand if you like movies |
| Stand if you like fast cars | Stand if you like sports | Stand if you like jewelry |

From top left: buyit/iStock/Thinkstock; imagephotography/iStock/Thinkstock; Creatas/Creatas/ThinkStock; Rawpixel Ltd/iStock/Thinkstock; Photodisc/Photodisc/Thinkstock; Fruit_Cocktail/iStock/Thinkstock

## The People Who Are Most Successful, Focus on What They Have in Common With Others

- The most successful heads of corporations are skilled at meeting people and, during the conversation, finding out and emphasizing what they both have in common.

- When you can make the amygdala of others feel good, they think that you like them.
- Conversely, when you accentuate things you don't have in common, it irritates the amygdala.
- The skill of identifying what you have in common with someone else can be developed through practice.

- Practice listening during conversations for anything a person says that you agree with or something they like that you also like.
- When you hear it, make sure to let the person know that you think the same way or like the same thing.

## Here Are a Couple Examples of How You Could Make the Amygdala Happy

*One student reads the dialog while the other student reads the dialog in italics.*

### Scenario 1

Why do you carry drumsticks in your back pocket?

*I play drums and when I am learning a new song, I air drum with my sticks.*

That's cool, I do the same thing with my fingers, I play lead guitar.

*I used to jam with friends all the time, then my mom moved here for work.*

I have some friends who all play guitar, and we sometimes hang out and just jam.

*You guys thinking about starting a band?*

Maybe. You should come over some time, and we'll check you out.

### Scenario 2

I see you boasting that Eagle gear. Is that your team?

*Yeah, I'm a diehard Eagle fan!*

Me too!

*Did you see the play on Sunday when . . .*

## Here Are a Couple Examples of How You Could Make the Amygdala Angry

### Scenario 1

Why do you carry drumsticks in your back pocket?

*I play drums and when I am learning a new song, I visualize playing with my sticks in the air.*

Don't you think you look crazy playing imaginary drums?

*No, I don't!*

I think I would look stupid doing that.

*If you think you look stupid, you probably do.*

You calling me stupid?

### Scenario 2

I see you boasting that Eagle gear. Is that your team?

*Yeah, I'm a diehard Eagle fan!*

You must like losing!

*Man, you need to shut up!*

## Let's Review the Three Skills to Help You Be More Successful

- Skill 1: Smile
- Skill 2: Greet
- Skill 3: Connect

This sounds simple, but if it is simple, why doesn't everybody do it? All skills take practice.

## The Only Way to Get Good at These Skills Is to Practice

- I want you all to be more successful. So this is what we are going to do.

- We are going to have a set time for everyone to practice.
- I will group two of you together.

  o Each of you will take turns starting a conversation.
  o Smile when you approach the person.
  o Greet them.
  o Then find out something you have in common.

- You are practicing for real-life situations.

  - Later in the year, there will be business people from the community coming in and doing interviews with you and letting you know how you did.

*It is not bad for students to do this exercise initially with students whom they like. However, once students are comfortable with the process, it is a good idea to pair them with students who are not like them or even students from a different class.*

In the initial paragraph of this chapter, it was mentioned that it is important to promote protective factors in a manner that will likely increase dopamine reinforcement by the brain. The following five-step outline merely incorporates the elements identified in the preceding chapter for designing an intervention so that there is dopamine reinforcement. The goal is that each time the students practice the skills, the following steps are incorporated. Remember, a behavior that is naturally reinforced by the brain will continue when external supports have ended.

### Step 1

- Designing a sequential action

  - Smile
  - Greet
  - Connect

### Step 2

- Make the action valued by the amygdala

  - The lesson established that the ability to connect to others is a predictor of *success* in life; reduce this to a sound bite that is repeated whenever the students engage in this action.

    o "We connect for success."

  - Success is a driving force of the amygdala.
  - Sound bite: "We connect for Success."

*Step 3*

- Visual cue to trigger the behavior

  - Whenever the following picture comes up on the board, it is time to practice our skills for success.

bombuscreative/iStock/Thinkstock

*Step 4*

- Consistent and predictable practice times

  o Once a week on Fridays, until every student has had an opportunity to participate in the exercise with every student in the class.

*Step 5*

- Reinforce the action

  - The teacher occasionally conducts games in class that incorporate how well students know one another. These games will motivate students in a fun way to find out things they have in common with their peers to do well whenever the games are played.
  - The teacher randomly passes out a prize to any student who demonstrated advanced knowledge of what they have in common with their peers.

    o The reward should be random to build anticipation.

*It is important to process with students after each exercise. Find out if the students were able to identify some things they had in common and what they were. Make sure students recognize that even when they know the purpose of the exercise, finding out what you have in common with someone else still makes them and the other person feel good.*

# 16

## The Education Revolution

The process of learning is an action that creates a range of reactions in the human brain. These reactions transform the brain in a manner no one could fathom in the past. The act of learning when done successfully creates a motivation for lifelong learning. It creates a rich tapestry for all future learning to connect and thrive.

What a student has learned in the past is predictive of what he or she will learn in the future. The brain tends to focus on and comprehend readily things related to what it has already learned. It takes only one teacher to spark an interest in reading, math, or science that will create a brain more able to focus on those subjects in the future. Students with parents who read to them regularly or do math with them create a student who comes to school with a brain more capable of focusing during story time or the math lesson.

However, all students do not come ready to learn, and what these students need is a skilled teacher. Students come with different genetic makeups and from various cultures, environments, and experiences that have shaped their brains either to learn more readily or to struggle academically. Students who come not ready to learn need a teacher who knows how to prime the brain to focus and how to get new information to the point of automation, which enables a world of advanced thought. A teacher who can take an advanced concept and transform it into an experience allows the brain to be aided by the body to enable students from assorted backgrounds the ability to gain a similar level of comprehension. A teacher who knows that higher-level thinking is not reserved for the most intelligent, but can be achieved by anyone if all the requirements that the brain demands are met.

Today's teachers must know that students are changing. Students today are born into a world that is so fast-paced and technologically advanced that the need for stimulation is merely a way of life. A true teacher is aware that nothing great has ever been accomplished without focus, pondering, and problem solving. Therefore, the skilled teacher embraces the new challenge of reshaping the brain to be able to focus.

The moment the student begins to focus, the unobtainable becomes obtainable. The student can not only learn but is also transformed. The student finds emotional stability in the fast-paced world. The brain begins to solidify connections that will infer emotional protection, physical strength, and cognitive longevity. At that moment, the teacher has become a healer.

As it relates to bullying, our students live in an environment in which seemingly benign things like their smartphones threaten to take a part of their humanity. Students are being robbed of the ability to care, the ability to feel the pain of another, or to find beauty in art. These students need teachers to guide them through the new technological age, embracing the advancements without becoming corrupted by them. Students need help navigating these new challenges. Narcissism is becoming common, no longer reserved for the most damaged individuals. The loss of empathy is creating a level of malice that is becoming commonplace. The age-old problem of bullying is finding a new breed of perpetrator. The best and the brightest are becoming willing participants. The physically weak are launching cruel attacks from the anonymity of their electronic devices.

Education can fill the gap by helping students learn that the loss of empathy is tantamount to losing their souls. They need to protect it to comprehend the world at a deep and meaningful level. Without empathy, they compromise the understanding of the spoken word. Most important, empathy is the foundation of our ability to preserve mankind.

Many of the world's greatest problems can be solved with simple steps. The obesity crisis requires us to eat the right things and move as nature intended. The unexpected outcome of the new age of the brain can be mitigated by just having moments of being unplugged and focusing on one thing. Our ability to understand one another at an intuitive level is restored by merely engaging in face-to-face communication. However, if the next generation is unaware that there is a problem, how can they defend against it?

In this moment, education might need to lead the revolution to protect the ever-adapting brains of children and adolescents. The brain is placid and able to recover quickly if consistent healthy practices are adopted. The key is consistency. A key element of learning is simply repetition. Repetition determines what the brain values. Consistent actions transform the brain and determine what is rewarding. Teachers equipped with a sound understanding of the brain and its many challenges can educate and transform through disciplined action.

The ability of an adult or system to adopt new behaviors and practice them consistently has historically been challenging for the educational system. However, the same science that gives us hope for the students gives us hope that adults and schools can change. Change begins with simple actions that have been proven through science to produce positive outcomes in the human brain. Educational systems need to establish and protect the time to practice these critical actions. Once these actions become repetitive, educators will begin to see the success students experience and be motivated to do more. Once the actions are valued, new behaviors will be reinforced and become habits and not chores.

The speed at which the outcomes identified in this book can be obtained is dramatically increased when the recommended strategies are implemented on a systemic level. *When an entire school embraces the strategies found in neuroscience and validated in longitudinal resiliency research, then tarnished reputations will be replaced by new perceptions.* Schools associated with failure will become schools that are desirable. The student who seeks to be successful in the world will desire to become a member of the school community. No longer is the old adage, *this is the way we have always done it*, satisfactory for students facing new obstacles. Education needs to embrace the new reality that schools must care for the whole child.

For the first time in the history of education, the inner workings of the human brain have gone beyond theory to practice. A majority of brain-compatible solutions validate numerous established education practices. There are a few neurological findings that require educators to slightly modify teaching practices to better align with current research. However, there are some crucial insights into the inner workings of the human brain that are foundational to students' evolving needs that require revolutionary change. These new issues require new solutions. The inability to institutionalize validated neuroscience practices related to school climate, instruction, and discipline can't continue to be explained away. Change is difficult, and education is justifiably slow to change to protect students from fads and gimmicks that could potentially harm them, but this rationalization is inconsistent with schools' embrace of technology. Many educators are encouraging the use of technologies in schools and classrooms without conducting studies on effectiveness and without consideration of unintended consequences. The reason that technology has been embraced is the level of comfort. Many teachers, like much of the general population, rely on their smartphones and cannot live without their iPads. They use technology so frequently that they cannot remember the time when they found technology frustrating to learn and difficult to use. The same level of comfort must be achieved with neuroscience for educators to embrace it. To achieve this level of comfort, a revolution must take place to saturate school climates, student discipline, and classroom instruction with neuroscience findings.

Implementing these changes will initially be met with some resistance. However, if educators struggle through the difficult fight, one day they will look back and know that the revolution was well worth the sacrifice. A revolution is needed because we can no longer wait for small incremental change when so much is at stake. The battle to transform instruction will maximize student learning. The fight is warranted because the physical and emotional health of our children is under attack. The revolution has to take place to secure the future of every student. In this brave new world, many fields such as neuroscience, medicine, management, psychology, and education are converging to support some specific theories that can no longer be ignored. Why wait until tomorrow to apply sound validated practices that we can implement today? Every educator has the ability to sound the alarm and strike a blow to make our education system the best it can possibly be. Viva la revolution!

*If you know the enemy and know yourself, you need not fear the result of a hundred battles. If you know yourself but not the enemy, for every victory gained you will also suffer a defeat. If you know neither the enemy nor yourself, you will succumb in every battle.*

— Sun Tzu, *The Art of War*

# References

Adler, N. E., Boyce, T., Chesney, M. A., Cohen, S., Folkman, S., Kahn, R. L., & Syme, S. L. (1994). Socioeconomic status and health. The challenge of the gradient. *American Psychologist, 49,* 15–24.

Ambady, N., & Rosenthal, R. (1992). Thin slices of expressive behavior as predictors of interpersonal consequences: A meta-analysis. *Psychological Bulletin, 111,* 256–274.

American Psychiatric Association. (2013). *Diagnostic and statistical manual of mental disorders* (5th ed.). Washington, DC: Author.

Bahrick, H. P., & Shelly, C. (1958). Time-sharing as an index of automatization. *Journal of Experimental Psychology, 56,* 288–293.

Baron-Cohen, S., Knickmeyer, R., & Belmonte, M. (2005). Sex differences in the brain: Implications for explaining autism. *Science, 310,* 819–823.

Bartholow, B. D., Bushman, B. J., & Sestir, M. A. (2006). Chronic violent video game exposure and desensitization: Behavioral and event-related brain potential data. *Journal of Experimental Social Psychology, 42,* 532–539.

Bédard, A., Lévesque, M., Bernier, P. J., & Parent, A. (2002). The rostral migratory stream in adult squirrel monkeys: Contribution of new neurons to the olfactory tubercle and involvement of the antiapoptotic protein Bcl-2. *European Journal of Neuroscience, 16,* 1917–1924.

Berenbaum, S. A., & Bailey, J. M. (2003). Effects on gender identity of prenatal androgens and genital appearance: Evidence from girls with congenital adrenal hyperplasia. *Journal of Clinical Endocrinology and Metabolism, 88,* 1102–1106.

Berkman, L. F. (1995). The role of social relations in health promotion. *Psychosomatic Medicine, 57,* 245–254.

Berridge, K. C. (2006). The debate over dopamine's role in reward: The case for incentive salience. *Psychopharmacology, 191*(3), 391–431.

Billington, J., Baron-Cohen, S., & Wheelwright, S. (2007). Cognitive style predicts entry into physical sciences and humanities: Questionnaire and performance tests of empathy and systemizing. *Learning and Individual Differences, 17,* 260–268.

Blachnio, A., & Weremko, M. (2011). Academic cheating is contagious: The influence of the presence of others on honesty. A study report. *International Journal of Applied Psychology, 1,* 14–19.

Blair, C. (2002). School readiness: Integrating cognition and emotion in a neurobiological conceptualization of child functioning at school entry. *American Psychologist, 57,* 111–127.

Bloom, B. S. (Ed). (1985). *Developing talent in young people.* New York, NY: Ballentine.

Blum, K. (1989). A commentary on neurotransmitter restoration as a common mode of treatment for alcohol, cocaine and opiate abuse. *Integrative Psychiatry, 6*, 199–204.

Boulware, M. I., Weick, J. P., Becklund, B. R., Kuo, S. P., Groth, R. D., & Mermelstein, P. G. (2005). Estradiol activates group I and II metabotropic glutamate receptor signaling, leading to opposing influences on cAMP response element-binding protein. *Journal of Neuroscience, 25*, 5066–5078.

Bransford, J. D. (1979). *Human cognition: Learning, understanding, and remembering.* Belmont, CA: Wadsworth.

Brotsky, S. R., & Giles, D. C. (2007). Inside the "pro-ana" community: A covert online participant observation. *Eating Disorders: The Journal of Treatment and Prevention, 15*, 93–109.

Brown v. Board of Education, 237 U.S. 483 (1954).

Buckner, R. L., Raichle, M. E., Miezin, F. M., & Petersen, S. E. (1996). Functional anatomic studies of memory retrieval for auditory words and visual pictures. *Journal of Neuroscience, 16*, 6219–6235.

Bunge, S. A., & Zelazo, P. D. (2006). A brain-based account of the development of rule use in childhood. *Current Directions in Psychological Science, 15*, 118–121.

Bushman, B. J., & Anderson, C. A. (2009). Comfortably numb: Desensitizing effects of violent media on helping others. *Psychological Science, 20*, 273–277.

Cannon, R. P., Schnall, S., & White, M. (2011). Transgressions and expressions: Affective facial muscle activity predicts moral judgements. *Social Psychological & Personality Science*, 325–331.

Carpenter, S. (2008). Buried prejudice. *Scientific American Mind, 19*, 33–39.

Carr E. G., McLaughlin D. M., Giacobbe-Greico T., & Smith C. E. (2003). Using mood ratings and mood induction in assessment and intervention for severe problem behavior. *American Journal on Mental Retardation, 108*, 32–55.

Carr, L., Iacoboni, M., Dubeau, M. C., Mazziotta, J. C., & Lenzi, G. L. (2003). Neural mechanisms of empathy in humans: A relay from neural systems for imitation to limbic areas. *Proceedings of the National Academy of Sciences, U.S.A., 100*, 5497–5502.

Carver, A. C., Livesey, D. J., & Charles, M. (2001). Further manipulation of the stop signal task: Developmental changes in the ability to inhibit responding with longer stop signal delays. *International Journal of Neuroscience, 111*, 39–53.

Castelli, D., Hillman, C., & Buck, S. (2007). Physical fitness and academic achievement in third- and fifth-grade students. *Journal of Sport & Exercise Psychology, 29*, 239–252.

Chapman, E., Baron-Cohen, S., Auyeung, B., Knickmeyer, R., Taylor, K., & Hackett, G. (2006). Fetal testosterone and empathy: Evidence from the empathy quotient (EQ) and the "Reading the Mind in the Eyes" test. *Social Neuroscience, 1*, 135–148.

Chatfield, T. (2010). *7 Ways games reward the brain* [Video]. Available from https://www.bmgi.com/big-ideas/research/tom-chatfield-7-ways-games-reward-brain

Chau, M., & Xu, J. (2007). *Studying customer groups from blogs.* Proceedings of the Sixth Workshop on E-Business (WEB2007), 200. Abstract retrieved from http://www.business.hku.hk/~mchau/papers/CustomerGroupsFromBlogs_WEB.pdf

Chiras, D. D. (2012). *Human body systems: Structure, function, and environment.* Burlington, MA: Jones & Bartlett Learning.

Cloninger, C. R. (1983). Genetic and environmental factors in the development of alcoholism. *Journal of Psychiatric Treatment Evaluation, 5,* 487–496.

Cohen, M. X. (2008). Neurocomputational mechanisms of reinforcement-guided learning in humans: A review. *Cognitive, Affective, and Behavioral Neuroscience, 8*(2), 113–125.

Cooke, S. F., & Bliss, T. V. P. (2006). Plasticity in the human nervous system. *Brain, 129*(7), 1659–1673.

Creer, D. J., Romberg, C., Saksida, L. M., van Praag, H., Bussey, T. J. (2010). Running enhances spatial pattern separation in mice. *Proceedings of the National Academy of Sciences, 107*(5), 2367–2372. doi:10.1073/pnas.0911725107

Cummings, E. E. (1994). *Complete poems, 1904–1962.* New York, NY: Liveright.

Davis IV, H., Liotti, M., Ngan, E. T., Woodward, T. S., Van Snellenberg, J. X., van Anders, S. M., . . . Mayberg, H.S. (2008). fMRI BOLD signal changes in elite swimmers when viewing videos of personal failure. *Brain Imaging and Behavior, 2,* 84–93.

DeThorne, L. S., & Schaefer, B. A. (2004). A guide to child nonverbal IQ measures. *American Journal of Speech-Language Pathology, 13,* 275–290.

Duggan, M. (2014). *Online harassment.* Washington, DC: Pew Research Center. Retrieved from www.pewinternet.org/2014/10/22/online-harassment/

Dygdon, J. A. (1998). Culture and lifestyle appropriate social skills intervention curriculum (CLASSIC): A program for socially valid social skills training (2d ed.). Austin, TX: PRO-ED.

Erickson, K. I., Prakash, R. S., Voss, M. W., Chaddock, L., Hu, L., Morris, K. S., White, S. M., . . . Kramer, A. F. (2009). Aerobic fitness is associated with hippocampal volume in elderly humans. *Hippocampus, 19,* 1030–1039.

Fang, F. C., Bennett, J. W., & Casadevall, A. (2013). Males are overrepresented among life science researchers committing scientific misconduct. *mBio, 4*(1), e00640-12. doi: 10.1128/mBio.00640-12

Fazio, R. H. (2014). Understanding implicit bias: How and when our actions fail to match our motivations. Invited presentation sponsored by the Implicit Bias Collaborative, The Women's Place at The Ohio State University, Columbus.

Ferreira, J. G., Tellez, L. A., Ren, X., Yeckel, C. W., de Araujo, I. E. (2012). Regulation of fat intake in the absence of flavour signalling. *Journal of Physiology, 590*(4), 953–972. doi: 10.1113/jphysiol.2011.218289

Firk, C., & Markus, C. R. (2009). Mood and cortisol responses following tryptophan-rich hydrolyzed protein and acute stress in healthy subjects with high and low cognitive reactivity to depression. *Clinical Nutrition, 28*(3), 266–271. doi: 10.1016/j.clnu.2009.03.002

Fletcher, P. C., Frith, C. D., Grasby, P. M., Shallice, T., Frackowiak, R. S. J., & Dolan, R. J. (1995). Brain systems for encoding and retrieval of auditory-verbal memory. *Brain, 118,* 401–416.

Fujioka, T., Ross, B., Kakigi, R., Pantev, C., & Trainor, L. J. (2006). One year of musical training affects development of auditory cortical-evoked fields in young children. *Brain, 129,* 2593–2608.

Funk, J. B., Baldacci, H. B., Pasold, T., & Baumgardner, J. (2004). Violence exposure in real-life, video games, television, movies, and the internet: Is there desensitization? *Journal of Adolescence, 27,* 23–39. doi: 10.1016/j. adolescence.2003.10.005

Gergen, K. J, Gergen, M. M., & Barton, W. H. (1973). Deviance in the dark. *Psychology Today, 7,* 129–131.

Gino, F., & Ariely, D. (2012). The dark side of creativity: Original thinkers can be more dishonest. *Journal of Personality and Social Psychology, 102,* 445–459. doi:10.1037/a0026406

Gino, F., Ayal, S., & Ariely, D. (2009). Contagion and differentiation in unethical behavior: The effect of one bad apple on the barrel. *Psychological Science, 20,* 393–398.

Gobet, F., & Simon, H. A. (1998). Expert chess memory: Revisiting the chunking hypothesis. *Memory, 6,* 225–255.

Godefroy, O., Lhullier, C., & Rousseaux, M. (1996). Non-spatial attention disorders in patients with frontal or posterior brain damage. *Brain, 119,* 191–202.

Gómez-Pinilla, F. (2008). Brain foods: The effects of nutrients on brain function. *Nature Reviews Neuroscience, 9,* 568–578.

Goold, C. P., & Nicoll, R. A. (2010). Single-cell optogenetic excitation drives homeostatic synaptic depression. *Neuron, 68,* 512–528.

Greenya, J. (2005). *Bullying: Are schools doing enough to stop the problem?* CQ Researcher. doi:http://dx.doi.org/10.4135/9781483349237.n18cqpress .com/cqresearcher/document.ph p?id=cqresrre2005020400&type=hitlist

Hamilton, J. (2008, Oct. 9). *Think you're multitasking? Think again.* Retrieved from http://www.npr.org/templates/story/story.php?storyId=95256794

Havas, D. A., Glenberg, A. M., Gutowski, K. A., Lucarelli, M. J., & Davidson, R. J. (2010). Cosmetic use of Botulinum Toxin-A affects processing of emotional language. *Psychological Science, 21,* 895–900. doi:10.1177/095679761 0374742

Hennenlotter, A., Dresel, C., Castrop, F., Ceballos-Baumann, A. O., Wohlschlager, A. M., & Haslinger, B. (2009). The link between facial feedback and neural activity within central circuitries of emotion—New insights from botulinum toxin-induced denervation of frown muscles. *Cerebral Cortex, 19,* 537–542.

Hensch, T. K. (2004). Critical period regulation. *Annual Review of Neuroscience, 27,* 549–579.

Hinrichs, P. (2010). The effects of the National School Lunch Program on education and health. *Journal of Policy Analysis and Management, 29*(3), 479–505. doi:10.1002/pam.20506

Hoek, H. W., & van Hoeken, D. (2003). Review of the prevalence and incidence of eating disorders. *International Journal of Eating Disorders, 34,* 383–396.

Hudson J. I., Hiripi E., Pope, H. G. Jr., & Kessler R. C. (2007). The prevalence and correlates of eating disorders in the National Comorbidity Survey Replication. *Biological Psychiatry, 61,* 348–358.

Ingwersen, J., Defeyter, M. A., Kennedy, D. O., Wesnes, K. A., & Scholey, A. B. (2007). A low glycaemic index breakfast cereal preferentially prevents children's cognitive performance from declining throughout the morning. *Appetite, 49,* 240–244.

Institute for Health Metrics and Evaluation. (2013). *The state of U.S. health: Innovations, insights, and recommendations from the Global Burden of Disease Study.* Seattle, WA: Author.

Inzlicht, M., Bartholow, B. D., & Hirsh, J. B. (2015). Emotional foundations of cognitive control. *Trends in Cognitive Sciences, 19,* 126–132.

Jha, A. P., Stanley, E. A., Kiyonaga, A., Wong, L., & Gelfand, L. (2010). Examining the protective effects of mindfulness training on working memory and affective experience. *Emotion, 10,* 54–64.

Johanson, D., & Edgar, B. (1996). *From Lucy to language.* New York, NY: Simon & Schuster.

Johnson, P. M., & Kenny, P. J. (2010). Dopamine D2 receptors in addiction-like reward dysfunction and compulsive eating in obese rats. *Nature Neuroscience, 13,* 635–641.

Johnson-Laird, P. (1983). *Mental models.* Cambridge, MA: Harvard University Press.

Keller, T. A., & Just, M. A. (2009). Altering cortical connectivity: Remediation-Induced changes in the white matter of poor readers. *Neuron, 64,* 624–631. doi: 10.1016/j.neuron.2009.10.018

Keys, A., Brožek, J., Henschel, A., Mickelsen, O., & Taylor, H. L. (1950). *The biology of human starvation* (2 volumes). St. Paul: University of Minnesota Press.

Kiecolt-Glaser, J. K., McGuire, L., Robles, T., & Glaser, R. (2002). Psycho-neuroimmunology: Psychological influences on immune function and health. *Journal of Consulting and Clinical Psychology, 70,* 537–547.

Kiesler, S., Siegel, J., & McGuire, T. W. (1984). Social psychological aspects of computer-mediated communication. *American Psychologist, 39,* 1123–1134.

Konrath, S., O'Brien, E., & Hsing, C. (2010). Changes in dispositional empathy in American college students over time: A meta-analysis. *Personality and Social Psychology, 15,* 180–198. Retrieved from http://dx.doi.org/10.1145/1180875.1180901

Kraus, N., & Chandrasekaran, B. (2010). Music training for the development of auditory skills. *Nature Reviews Neuroscience, 11,* 599–605.

Kuhl, P. (2011). Early language learning and literacy: Neuroscience implications for education. *Mind, Brain, and Education, 5,* 128–142. Retrieved from http://www.ncbi.nlm.nih.gov/pubmed/21892359

Kuhl, P. K., Coffey-Corina, S., Padden, D., & Dawson, G. (2005). Links between social and linguistic processing of speech in preschool children with autism: Behavioral and electro-physiological evidence. *Developmental Science, 8,* 1–12.

LaBerge, D., & Samuels, S. J. (1974). Toward a theory of automatic information processing in reading. *Cognitive Psychology, 6,* 293–323.

Lajoie, G., McLellan, A., & Seddon, C. (2001). *Take action against bullying.* Coquitlam, B.C., Canada: Bully B'ware Productions.

LeDoux, J. E. (1996). *The emotional brain.* New York, NY: Simon & Schuster.

Leon-Carrion, J., García-Orza, J., & Pérez-Santamaría, F. J. (2004). Development of the inhibitory component of the executive functions in children and adolescents. *International Journal of Neuroscience, 114,* 1291–1311.

Levine, S. (2008). *School lunch politics: The surprising history of America's favorite welfare program.* Princeton, NJ: Princeton University Press.

Lozoff, B., De Andraca, I., Castillo, M., Smith, J., Walter, T., & Pino, P. (2003). Behavioral and developmental effects of preventing iron-deficiency anemia in healthy full-term infants. *Pediatrics, 112,* 846–854.

Luders, E., Kurth, F., Mayer, E. A., Toga, A. W., Narr, K. L., & Gaser, C. (2012). The unique brain anatomy of meditation practitioners: Alterations in cortical gyrification. *Frontiers in Human Neuroscience, 6,* 34. doi:10.3389/fnhum.2012.00034

Lutchmaya, S., Baron-Cohen, S., & Raggatt, P. (2002). Foetal testosterone and eye contact in 12-month-old human infants. *Infant Behavior and Development, 25,* 327–335.

Lutz, A., Slagter, H. A., Dunne, J., & Davidson, R. J. (2008). Attention regulation and monitoring in meditation. *Trends in Cognitive Sciences, 12,* 163–169.

Malamuth, N., Linz, D., & Yao, M. (2005). The Internet and aggression: Motivation, disinhibitory and opportunity aspects. In Y. Amichai-Hamburger (Ed.), *The social net: Understanding human behavior in cyberspace* (pp. 163–190). New York, NY: Oxford University Press.

Malterer, M. B., Lilienfeld, S. O., Neumann, C. S., & Newman, J. P. (2009). Concurrent validity of the psychopathic personality inventory with offender and community samples. *Assessment, 17,* 3–15.

Martinson, B. C., Anderson, M. S., & de Vries, R. (2005). Scientists behaving badly. *Nature, 435,* 737–738.

McCabe, D. L., & Treviño, L. K. (1997). Individual and contextual influences on academic dishonesty: A multicampus investigation. *Research in Higher Education, 38,* 379–396.

McGee, M. G., & Wilson, D. W. (1984). *Psychology: Science and application.* St. Paul, MN: West.

Medeiros-Ward, N., Watson, J. M., & Strayer, D. L. (2012). Supertaskers and the multitasking brain. *Scientific American Mind, 23,* 22–29.

Meltzoff, A. N., Kuhl, P. K., Movellan, J., & Sejnowski, T. (2009). Foundations for new science of learning. *Science, 17,* 284–288.

Miles, L. K., Karpinska, K., Lumsden, J., & Macrae, C. N. (2010). The meandering mind: Vection and mental time travel. *PLoS ONE* 5(5), e10825. doi:10.1371/journal.pone.0010825

Mirsky, S. (2008, December 3). The science of pain [Audio podcast]. Retrieved from http://www.scientificamerican.com/podcast/episode/the-science-of-pain-08-12-03/

Morgan, T. J. H., Uomini, N. T., Rendell, L. E., Chouinard-Thuly, L., Street, S. E., Lewis, H. M., . . . Laland, K. N. (2015). Experimental evidence for the co-evolution of hominin tool-making teaching and language. *Nature Communications, 6,* 6029.

Munakata, Y., Herd, S. A., Chatham, C. H., Depue, B. E., Banich, M. T., & O'Reilly, R. C. (2011). A unified framework for inhibitory control. *Trends in Cognitive Sciences, 15,* 453–459.

The National Center on Addiction and Substance Abuse at Columbia University. (2011). The importance of family dinners VII. Retrieved from http://www.centeronaddiction.org/addiction-research/reports/importance-of-family-dinners-2011.

Neville, H. J. (Executive Producer), Marquez, A. (Producer/Director), Taylor, P. (Producer), & Pakulak, E. (Producer). (2009). *Changing brains: Effects of experience on human brain development* [Motion picture]. Eugene: University of Oregon.

Niedenthal, P. M., Winkielman, P., Mondillon, L., & Vermeulen, N. (2009). Embodied emotion concepts. *Journal of Personality and Social Psychology, 96,* 120–136.

Núñez, R. E., & Sweetser, E. (2006). With the future behind them: Convergent evidence from Aymara language and gesture in the crosslinguistic comparison of spatial construals of time. *Cognitive Science, 30,* 1–49.

Ophir, E., Nass, C. I., & Wagner, A. D. (2009). Cognitive control in media multitaskers. *Proceedings of the National Academy of Sciences, 106,* 15583–15587. doi: 10.1073/pnas.0903620106

Pea, R., Nass, C., Meheula, L., Rance, M., Kumar, A., Bamford, H., . . . Zhou, M. (2012). Paper media use, face-to-face communication, media multitasking, and social well-being among 8 to 12 year old girls. *Developmental Psychology, 48,* 327–336. doi:10.1037/a0027030

Peterson, R. (2005). Investing lessons from neuroscience: fMRI of the reward system. *Brain Research Bulletin, 67,* 391–397.

Plessy v. Ferguson, 163 U.S. 537 (1896).

Popkin, B. M. (2006). Global nutrition dynamics: The world is shifting rapidly toward a diet linked with noncommunicable diseases. *American Journal of Clinical Nutrition, 84,* 289–298.

Porter, S., Fairweather, D., Drugge, J., Herve, H., Birt, A. R., & Boer, D. P. (2000). Profiles of psychopathy in incarcerated sexual offenders. *Criminal Justice & Behavior, 27,* 216–233.

Preston, S. D., & de Waal, F. B. M. (2002). Empathy: Its ultimate and proximate bases. *Behavioral and Brain Sciences, 25,* 1–72.

Puig, M. V., & Miller, E. K. (2012). The role of prefrontal dopamine D1 receptors in the neural mechanisms of associative learning. *Neuron, 74,* 874–886.

Rampersaud, G. C., Pereira, M. A., Girard, B. L., Adams, J., & Metzl, J. D. (2005). Breakfast habits, nutritional status, body weight, and academic performance in children and adolescents. *Journal of the American Dietetic Association, 105,* 743–760.

Rauscher, F. H., Shaw, G. L., & Ky, K. N. (1993). Music and spatial task performance. *Nature, 365*(6447), 611.

Robertson, I. H. (2012). *The winner effect: How power affects your brain.* London, England: Bloomsbury.

Robinson, A. L., Heaton, R. K., Lehman, R. A., & Stilson, D. W. (1980). The utility of the Wisconsin Card Sorting Test in detecting and localizing frontal lobe lesions. *Journal of Consulting and Clinical Psychology, 48,* 605–614.

Ruby, P., & Decety, J. (2004). How would you feel versus how do you think she would feel? A neuroimaging study of perspective-taking with social emotions. *Journal of Cognitive Neuroscience, 16,* 988–999.

Rudge, P., & Warrington, E. K. (1991). Selective impairment of memory and visual perception in splenial tumors. *Brain, 114,* 349–360.

Sanchez, E., Robertson, T. R., Lewis, C. M., Rosenbluth, B., Bohman, T., & Casey, D. M. (2001). Preventing bullying and sexual harassment in elementary schools: The expect respect model. In R. A. Geffner, M. Loring, & C. Young (Eds.), *Bullying behavior: Current issues, research, and interventions* (pp. 157–180). New York, NY: Haworth Maltreatment & Trauma Press.

Schultz, W. (2007). Behavioral dopamine signals. *Trends in Neuroscience, 30,* 203–210.

Skipper, J. I., Goldin-Meadow, S., Nusbaum, H. C., & Small, S. L. (2009). Gestures orchestrate brain networks for language understanding. *Current Biology, 19,* 661–667.

Small, G, & Moody, T. (2009). Your brain on Google: Patterns of cerebral activation during Internet searching. *American Journal of Geriatric Psychiatry, 17,* 116–126.

Snedeker, J., Geren, J., & Shafto, C. (2007). Starting over: International adoption as a natural experiment in language development. *Psychological Science, 18,* 79–87.

Spitzer, M., Fischbacher, U., Herrnberger, B., Grön, G., & Fehr, E. (2007). The neural signature of social norm compliance. *Neuron, 56,* 185–196.

Srinivasan, S., Sadegh, L., Elle, I. C., Christensen, A. G., Faergeman, N. J., & Ashrafi, K. (2008). Serotonin regulates C. elegans fat and feeding through independent molecular mechanisms. *Cell Metababolism, 7,* 533–544.

Steen, R. G. (2011). Retractions in the scientific literature: Is the incidence of research fraud increasing? *Journal of Medical Ethics 37,* 249–253.

Stice, E., Yokum, S., Blum, K., & Bohon, C. (2010). Weight gain associated with reduced striatal response to palatable food. *Journal of Neuroscience, 30,* 13105–13109.

Stice, E., Yokum, S., Bohon, C., Marti, N., & Smolen, A. (2010). Reward circuitry responsivity predicts weight gain: Moderating effects of DRD2 and DRD4. *NeuroImage, 50,* 1618–1625.

Sylvester, C., Voelkl, J. E., & Ellis, G. D. (2001). *Therapeutic recreation programming: Theory and practice.* State College, PA: Venture.

Teicher, M. H., Samson, J. A., & Polcari, A., & McGreenery, C. E. (2006). Sticks, stones, and hurtful words: Relative effects on various forms of childhood maltreatment. *American Journal of Psychiatry, 163,* 993–1000.

Thomaes, S., Bushman, B. J., Orobio de Castro, B., & Stegge, H. (2009). What makes narcissists bloom? A framework for research on the etiology and development of narcissism. *Development and Psychopathology, 21,* 1233–1247.

Twenge, J. M. (2006). *Generation me: Why today's young Americans are more confident, assertive, entitled—and more miserable than ever before.* New York, NY: Free Press.

Uchino, B. N. (2004). *Social support and physical health outcomes: Understanding the health consequences of our relationships.* New Haven, CT: Yale University Press.

Uchino, B. N. (2009). Understanding the links between social support and physical health: A lifespan perspective with emphasis on the separability of perceived and received support. *Perspectives in Psychological Science, 4,* 236–255.

Valenstein, E., Bowers, D., Verfaellie, M., Heilman, K. M., Day, A., & Watson, R. T. (1987). Retrosplenial amnesia. *Brain, 110,* 1631–1646.

Van Dijk, T. A., & Kintsch, W. (1983). *Strategies of discourse comprehension.* New York, NY: Academic Press.

Vance, E., & Sanchez, H. (1998). *Creating a service system that builds resiliency.* Raleigh: North Carolina Division of Mental Health, Developmental Disabilities, and Substance Abuse Services. Retrieved from http://www.telability.org/handouts/risk-resiliency-vance.pdf

Volkow, N. D., Chang, L., Wang, G. J., Fowler, J. S., Leonido-Yee, M., Franceschi, D., . . . Miller, E. N. (2001). Dopamine transporter losses in methamphetamine abusers are associated with psychomotor impairment. *American Journal of Psychiatry, 158,* 377–382.

Wansink, B., & Johnson, K. A. (2015). The clean plate club: About 92% of self-served food is eaten. *International Journal of Obesity, 39,* 371–374. doi: 10.1038/ijo.2014.104

Wardle, J., & Cooke, L. (2008). Genetic and environmental determinants of children's food preferences. *British Journal of Nutrition, 99,* S15–S21.

Wesselmann, E. D., Butler, F. A., Williams, K. D., & Pickett, C. L. (2010). Adding injury to insult: Unexpected rejection leads to more aggressive responses. *Aggressive Behavior, 36,* 232–237.

Whitmore, J., & Maker, C. (1985). *Intellectual giftedness in disabled persons.* Rockville, MD: Aspen.

Williams, B. R., Ponesse, J. S., Schachar, R. J., Logan, G. D., & Tannock, R. (1999). Development of inhibitory control across the life span. *Developmental Psychology 35,* 205–213.

Williams, K. D., Cheung, C. K. T., & Choi, W. (2000). Cyberostracism: Effects of being ignored over the Internet. *Journal of Personality and Social Psychology, 79,* 748–762.

Wurtman, R. J., & Wurtman, J. J. (1989). Carbohydrates and depression. *Scientific American, 260*(1), 68–75.

# Index

Note: Page numbers in *italic* refer to illustrations.

**CORWIN** A SAGE Publishing Company

Helping educators make the greatest impact

**CORWIN HAS ONE MISSION:** to enhance education through intentional professional learning.

We build long-term relationships with our authors, educators, clients, and associations who partner with us to develop and continuously improve the best evidence-based practices that establish and support lifelong learning.

# Solutions you want. Experts you trust. Results you need.

Printed in the USA
CPSIA information can be obtained
at www.ICGtesting.com
LVHW081341240923
758982LV00003B/6